Paradise
Factor

Paradise Factor

GEORGE and MEG PATTERSON

Healing an Addicted Society

WORD PUBLISHING
Nelson Word Ltd
Milton Keynes, England
WORD AUSTRALIA
Kilsyth, Australia
WORD COMMUNICATIONS LTD
Vancouver, B.C., Canada
STRUIK CHRISTIAN BOOKS (PTY) LTD
Cape Town, South Africa
JOINT DISTRIBUTORS SINGAPORE –
ALBY COMMERCIAL ENTERPRISES PTE LTD
and
CAMPUS CRUSADE, ASIA LTD
PHILIPPINE CAMPUS CRUSADE FOR CHRIST
Quezon City, Philippines
CHRISTIAN MARKETING NEW ZEALAND LTD
Havelock North, New Zealand
JENSCO LTD
Hong Kong
SALVATION BOOK CENTRE
Malaysia

THE PARADISE FACTOR

Copyright © 1994 by George and Meg Patterson.

Published by Nelson Word Ltd., Milton Keynes, England, 1994.

ISBN 0-85009-533-6   (Australia ISBN 1-86258-151-7)

Scripture quotations are from the following sources:
    The King James Version of the Bible.
    The New King James Version (NKJV), copyright © 1985 by Thomas Nelson, Inc.
    The New International Version (NIV), copyright © 1973, 1978, 1984 by International Bible Society.
    The Good News Bible (GNB), copyright © American Bible Society, New York, 1966, 1971, 1976.

Reproduced, printed and bound in Great Britain for Nelson Word Ltd. by Cox and Wyman Ltd., Reading.

94 95 96 97 / 10 9 8 7 6 5 4 3 2 1

ACKNOWLEDGEMENTS

*I*t would be an impossible task to list all who have contributed towards the material contained in this book. As will be seen it is a collection of meditation and memories of books read, poems recalled, thoughts accumulated, and sermons preached. Where possible we have recorded the names of people or books or incidents. To them, and the many forgotten by the passage of years—but whose contribution to our lives is remembered with great pleasure— we express our deep appreciation.

We also wish to acknowledge the help provided by the various versions of the Bible used in the book: the *King James Authorised*, the *New King James Version*, the *New International Version*, the *Good News Bible*, sometimes used in combination in the interest of the context.

Finally, we wish to acknowledge as always the great help of the London Library, and the Evangelical Library, in providing facilities for research.

. . . that blessed mood,
In which the burthen of the mystery,
In which the heavy and the weary weight,
Of all this unintelligible world,
Is lightened:—that serene and blessed mood,
In which the affections gently lead us on,—
Until the breath of this corporeal frame
And even the motion of our human blood
Almost suspended, we are laid asleep
In body, and become a living soul:
While with an eye made quiet by the power
Of harmony, and the deep power of joy,
We see into the life of things . . .

. . . And I have felt
A presence that disturbs me with the joy
Of elevated thoughts; a sense sublime
Of something far more deeply interfused
Whose dwelling is the light of setting suns,
And the round ocean and the living air,
And the blue sky, and in the mind of man:
A motion and a spirit, that impels
All thinking things, all objects of all thought,
And rolls through all things . . .

William Wordsworth:
Lines from Above Tintern Abbey

CONTENTS

GEORGE'S PREFACE

I went to Tibet in 1947 and lived there for three years.[1] Two of my most profound experiences occurred when I was there: one was to be confronted by parapsychological phenomena beyond my Western and Christian education; and the other was to read *The Tibetan Book of the Dead*. I continued to live on the borders of Tibet for another eleven years, studying and writing, working my way to a closer and deeper understanding of the ways of God in the world.

Several years later I was a member of a television team making several TV documentaries in Asia, two of which were *Raid into Tibet*—an account of Tibetan guerrillas attacking Chinese military convoys inside Tibet—and *The Opium Trail*—an account of the drug traffic from the 'Golden Triangle' of Burma, Laos and Thailand to Hong Kong. Following these activities I was invited to give a series of lectures in the United States, on the subjects of the Tibetan revolt against China and the drug trafficking from the Far East.

I arrived in the United States at the height of the late 1960s youth revolt spreading from Europe, and the rock music explosion from Britain led by the Beatles, the Rolling Stones, The Who, Cream and Led Zeppelin. The unparalleled political and social protest movement was challenging every accepted practice in Western societies, and the focus of the revolt was the demand for a better world led by better people; for a world of spiritual values—freedom, love, peace and joy—and not just material ambitions.

Ironically and tragically, those who provided the articulation of these paradisal hungers—the rock musicians— like the politicians they despised, had neither experience nor knowledge of how to realise them, and they led the way by default into the illusionary counterfeits of drugs, oriental mysticism and the occult.

---

1. See *Requiem for Tibet*, George N. Patterson (London: Aurum Press, 1990)

Two hundred years of secular democracy and secular humanism, launched by the 'Age of Reason', looked like being swept away by a generation of disillusioned youth who had rediscovered 'the mystic religious experience'. Then Dr Timothy Leary of Harvard University showed them how it was possible to rediscover paradise without any religious epiphanies, but simply and chemically with 300 millionths of a gram of LSD. Books, magazines and newspapers described what it was like to 'be one with the universe', to 'exist on a multitude of levels and not just of the puny one called I'. So many things happened in the 'paradisal psychedelic state' they could not be expressed in everyday language, and new terms and definitions were devised to accommodate them. After being thrown out of Harvard because of his advocacy of drug-taking, Dr Timothy Leary opened a psychedelic retreat in upstate New York, where he catered for all those wishing to explore 'the other world'.

When it became known that I had lived in Tibet for three years, on the borders of Tibet for eleven more years, spoke the language, had written and broadcast and lectured on Tibetan tantric practices, and on political revolution and the drug explosion in Asia, I was inundated with requests to lecture on these and related topics. Not only had I read *The Tibetan Book of the Dead* in the original language, I had observed and experienced the phenomena at first hand.

I had also met the theosophist guru of the psychedelic movement, Lama Anagarika Govinda, an Austrian who claimed to be a leading interpreter of Tibetan Buddhism, and who became a teacher of Leary and his associates. Like the Tibetans, I had not been impressed by Govinda, but he was the dominant religious figure of the protest movement of the time, postulating 'the grand design' of infiltrating the West with oriental philosophy. 'You,' Govinda said to Leary, with more flattery than insight, 'are the predictable result of a strategy that has been unfolding for over fifty years . . . You have been the unwitting tool of the great transformation of our age.'

Other Europeans, with borrowed Indian and Tibetan names, became the leaders of what was to become known as 'the dawning of the Age of Aquarius'. One of them, Sri Krishna Prem, alias Ronald Nixon, told Leary:

> Over the centuries our Hindu philosophers have seen everything come and go. Empires, religions, famines, good times, invasions, reforms, liberations, repressions. And drugs. Drugs are among the most influential and dangerous powers available to humans. They open up glorious and pleasurable chambers in the mind. They give great power. Thus they can seduce the searcher away from the Path.

Among the intellectual leaders in the West advocating the use of chemicals to induce a spiritual experience was Aldous Huxley. I met him in London in the early 1960s, together with Rosalind Heywood of the Psychical Research Society; Eileen Garrett, the famous medium and cofounder with Professor J. B. Rhind of parapsychology centres; Naomi Mitchison, and Prince Peter of Greece and Denmark and his mother Princess Marie Bonaparte (a lifetime confidante of Sigmund Freud), who were all interested in 'parapsychological phenomena'. Huxley at the time was experimenting with the drug mescaline, the findings of which he later published as *Doors of Perception*. He wrote:

> . . . mescaline or some other chemical substance may play a part by making it possible for young people to 'taste and see' what they have learned at second hand, or directly but at a lower level of intensity, in the writings of the religious, or the works of poets, painters and musicians.

Huxley described his first experience of mescaline as being like 'passing through a screen and suddenly seeing what

Adam had seen on the first morning of creation'. It was as though, born myopic, he had just had his first pair of spectacles. He had seen 'eternity in a flower, infinity in four chair legs, and the Absolute in the folds of a pair of trousers'. Mescaline, he told his editor, was 'the most extraordinary and significant experience available to human beings this side of the Beatific Vision'.

Writing to his friend, Humphrey Osmond, he enclosed the ditty:

> To make this trivial world sublime
> Take half a gramme of phanerothyme.

In reply Osmond wrote sardonically:

> To fathom hell or soar angelic
> Just take a pinch of psychedelic.

Others of Leary's associates were also sceptical of his wilder essays into 'the other world', and its possibilities for this world. One of them, David McClelland, wrote:

> It is probably no accident that the society which most consistently encouraged the use of these substances, India, produced one of the sickest social orders ever created by mankind, in which thinking men spent their time lost in the Buddha position under the influence of drugs expanding consciousness, while poverty, disease, social discrimination, and superstition reached their highest and most organised form in all history.

One of the leading philosophers and writers of the 'drug mystic movement' was Alan Watts, an Anglican clergyman who had become a Buddhist. One Easter he organised a psychedelic religious ceremony in Leary's house, composed of readings from the New Testament and other literature. The 'sacrament' was LSD, served in goblets, with French bread.

Leary was envious of the sophisticated Watts and he, in turn, organised a chemical religious ceremony with twenty divinity students in Boston University's Marsh Chapel. Half of the students were provided with the chemical psilocybin, and half with nicoturic acid. There was total chaos as the members staggered around in a drugged haze, some moaning, some fixating on the religious icons, some playing weird music, as they experienced various kinds of mystic euphoria. It became known as 'the miracle of Marsh Chapel'.

In their book, *The Drug Beat*, the authors Allen Geller and Maxwell Boas recorded:

> Three hundred to six hundred micrograms of LSD take the individual to the profound levels of what has been termed the religious or mystical experience. In this state he may feel 'a great love for all things in the cosmos', and 'a oneness with God' . . . an illumination similar to Zen Satori, and a sense of complete psychological integration . . .

Then there was the Indian Maharishi, selling cheap 'cosmic consciousness' as 'transcendental meditation'. Leary's 'four evangelists'—the Beatles—launched the small and giggling yogi on the world's stage in 1967 when they went to India to be 'enlightened'. Within three months they had become disillusioned when they admitted reluctantly, 'He's human. We thought at first he wasn't.'

I met the Maharishi in Hollywood where we were both the featured participants in a celebrity gathering; the Maharishi to talk about transcendental meditation, and I to talk about Tibetan occultism. During the course of his remarks the Maharishi said a number of things about Christianity that were not true—and some things about Hinduism that were questionable. While living in India I had for several years been the house-guest and close friend of the noted Tagore family in both Santineketan and Kalimpong and from them and their distinguished circle of friends and acquaintances I had learned basic Hindu teachings. What the Maharishi was propounding at times was considerably at variance from these—and to make matters worse, when challenged, he replied only with an inane, high-pitched giggle.

But his audience loved it. Famous film stars, diplomats, businessmen, professional people, scholars, all sat around wide-eyed as he trotted out a Hindu platitude they would never have accepted had it been delivered by a Western Christian priest or pastor. But this oriental guru promised them a quick and easy paradisal cosmic consciousness. Twenty years later, the Maharishi was taking a two-page spread in the prestigious journals and newspapers to advertise:

Maharishi Offers Every Government
ALLIANCE WITH NATURE'S GOVERNMENT
Through Maharishi's Vedic Science and Technology
TO CREATE HEAVEN ON EARTH.

Meanwhile Leary and his associates were competing to stay in the lead in promising paradisal experiences. He advocated altering the US constitution to include 'a fifth freedom'. This was the freedom to do what one wished with one's own consciousness. Congress, he maintained, should make no law to abridge the individual's right to seek an expanded consciousness. This fifth freedom was necessary, he argued, to permit selective use of psychedelic drugs 'to enable Americans to recover a spiritual dimension that would free them to do great things—explore the stars, conquer disease, eliminate poverty'.

He proposed a new organisation, the International Foundation for Internal Freedom, IFIF for short, which would be composed of a multitude of autonomous cells, each constructed around an IFIF-trained guide in chemical religious mysticism. These cells would multiply until they covered the world. Writing about this in his book, *Storming Heaven*, Jay Stevens said:

> Indeed the debate over mind-drugs threatened to overtake the Harvard-Yale game as a topic of undergraduate small-talk. The street price of a sugar cube laced with LSD was said to be five dollars, and, if you believed the rumours, every third person in Harvard Square had them for sale.
>
> . . . A few days later the (Harvard) *Crimson* carried a response from Leary and Alpert, which brushed aside the question of health hazards to focus on the Fifth Freedom. 'A major civil liberties issue of the next decade will be the control and expansion of consciousness,' they warned. 'Who controls your cortex? Who decides on the range and limit of your awareness? If you want to research your own nervous system, expand your consciousness, who is to decide you can't and why?' . . .

The Harvard *Crimson* gave its reporter's version of the IFIF's activities:

> The shoddiness of their work as scientists is the result less of incompetence than of a conscious rejection of scientific ways of looking at things. Leary and Alpert fancy themselves prophets of a psychic revolution designed to free Western man from the limitations of consciousness as we know it. They are contemptuous of all organised systems of action—of what they call the 'roles' and 'games' of society. They prefer mystical ecstasy to the fulfilment available through work, politics, religion and creative art.

A more serious attempt to define consciousness and the mystical was conducted by Jean Houston of the Foundation of

Mind Research. Investigating the effects of LSD and other means of expanding consciousness she defined the ultimate experience as the *mysterium*, or 'the source level of reality', 'primordial essence', 'the ultimate ground of being'. She elaborated:

> Another aspect of the experience is in the subject becoming aware of himself as continuous with the energy of the universe. It is frequently described with words to the effect that the subject was part of a dynamic continuum. It is also experienced as a state in which the subject professes to being filled by divinity . . .

In a joint book with Robert Masters, *The Varieties of Psychedelic Experience*, they divided the unconscious into four categories: (i) sensory; (ii) recollective-analytic; (iii) symbolic; (iv) integral. The *sensory* level was peopled with vivid images of persons, animals, landscapes, architecture, mythical creatures. The *recollective-analytical*—the region most familiar to psychotherapy—was most responsive to LSD, as was the sensory. The *symbolic* level contained the historically recognised 'archetypes' recorded by Freud and Jung. The *integral* level was the most obscure and difficult to penetrate, described as 'a confrontation with the Ground of Being, God . . . Essence or Fundamental Reality'.

Writing about the close association between chemicals— particularly alcohol in his context—and the realm of the spiritual in the unconscious, William James, the noted author of *The Varieties of Religious Experience*, said:

> The sway of alcohol over mankind is unquestionable, due to its power to stimulate the mystical faculties of human nature, usually crushed to earth by the cold facts and dry criticisms of the sober hour. Sobriety

diminishes, discriminates and says no; drunkenness expands, unites and says yes. It is, in fact, the great exciter of the Yes factor in man. It brings its votary from the chill periphery of things to the radiant core. It makes him for the moment one with truth. Not through mere perversity do men run after it . . . The drunken consciousness is one bit of the mystic consciousness and our total opinion of it must find its place in our opinion of the larger whole.

Nitrous oxide and ether, especially nitrous oxide, when sufficiently diluted with air, stimulate the mystical consciousness in an extraordinary degree. Depth upon depth of truth seems revealed to the inhaler. This truth fades out, however, or escapes, at the moment of coming to; and if any words remain over in which it seemed to clothe itself, they prove to be the veriest nonsense. Nevertheless, the sense of a profound meaning having been there persists . . .

Aldous Huxley, despite his advocacy of chemicals to stimulate the spiritual experience, stated similar conclusions more succinctly and exactly when he wrote, in *Doors of Perception*:

Psychic experiences which do not contribute to sanctification are not experiences of God but merely of certain unfamiliar aspects of the psychophysical universe . . . Where there is no evidence of sanctification, there is no reason to suppose that the experience has anything to do with God.

Both Old and New Testaments contained evidence of

the close association between the chemical and the spiritual, but clearly distinguished the one from the other. After the destruction of the ancient world by the Flood, the righteous, but seemingly unsuspecting, Noah got drunk on his own home-grown wine, and brought disgrace to his family. After the destruction of Sodom the fleeing unrighteous Lot got drunk and committed incest with his daughters. Solomon said that he gave himself to both wine and wisdom, and gave the fruits of both experiences in the books of Proverbs and Ecclesiastes. In the Song of Solomon the Bride says of the Bridegroom: 'Your love is better than wine.' And Jeremiah said of the prophets: 'My heart is broken within me; all my bones tremble. I am like a drunken man, like a man overcome with wine; because of the Lord and his holy words.' Peter and the other apostles were thought to be 'drunk with new wine', when filled with Holy Spirit. And Paul said: 'Be not drunk with wine, but be filled with the Spirit.'

That chemicals should be able to provide any essential wisdom was dismissed as ridiculous by Arthur Koestler in the book he edited, *Beyond Reductionism*:

> . . . It is fundamentally wrong, and naive, to expect that drugs can present the mind with gratis gifts—put into it something which is not already there. Neither mystic insights, nor philosophic wisdom, nor creative power, can be provided by pill or injection. The psychopharmacist cannot *add* to the faculties of the brain—but he can, at best, *eliminate* obstructions and blockages which impede their proper use. He cannot aggrandise us—but he can, within limits, normalise us; he cannot put additional circuits within the brain, but he can, again within limits, improve the coordination between existing ones, attenuate conflicts, prevent the blowing of fuses, and ensure a steady power supply. That is all the help we can ask for—but if we were able to attain it, the benefits for mankind would be incalculable . . .

Why do Hong Kong, with almost six million areligious Chinese, and the United States, with eighty million evangelical Christians, have, proportionately, the worst drug problems in the world? Why do over one billion Chinese Marxists have no major addictions (although they have the worst nicotine problem in the world) while Soviet and Eastern European Marxists have monumental alcohol and other addictions? Why is Buddhist meditation in Thailand so successful in addictions (although 90 per cent of the addicts return to their drug before they can begin the successful meditation)? Why does an authoritarian and ascetic religion like Islam have so many alcohol and heroin addicts in areas such as Indonesia, Pakistan and Iran? What is the link between chemical and behavioural addictions and the realm of the spiritual?

Living in Asia for thirty years, I was fascinated by these and other questions. Eventually, when Meg, my wife, became involved in researching NeuroElectric Therapy (NET), we both concluded that, while it would take several books to demonstrate answers to some if not all of them, the most significant feature in all addictions was 'the Paradise Factor', that indescribable experience which hovers at the edge of consciousness and can never be forgotten. This book is an attempt by Meg and me, out of our combined experiences, to describe the indescribable, and to bring it within the reach of all.

CHAPTER 1

The Hunger for Transcendence

*T*he 'Paradise Factor' is when an individual discovers a sensation of pleasure beyond any previous experience, and then forever afterwards is tantalised by the memory. It is when a baby discovers its mother's breast, a child discovers the taste of an ice cream, an adolescent discovers sex, an adult discovers love, a sinner discovers salvation—and an addict discovers drugs.

C. S. Lewis, in his book, *Surprised by Joy*, describes three separate events in his life which precipitated the experience:

> The first is itself the memory of a memory. As I stood beside a flowering currant bush on a summer day there suddenly arose in me without warning . . . the memory of that earlier morning at the Old House, when my brother had brought his toy garden into the nursery. It is difficult to find words strong enough for the sensation which came over me; Milton's 'enormous bliss' of Eden . . . comes somewhere near it . . . It had taken only a moment of time; and in a certain sense everything else that had ever happened to me was insignificant in comparison . . .
>
> The second glimpse came through *Squirrel Nutkin* . . . It sounds fantastic to say that one

can be enamoured of a season, but that is something like what happened; and, as before, the experience was one of intense desire . . . In this experience also there was the same surprise and the same sense of incalculable importance. It was something quite different from ordinary life and even from ordinary pleasure; something, as they would now say, 'in another dimension . . .'

The third glimpse came through poetry. I had become fond of Longfellow's *Saga of King Olaf*; fond of it in a casual, shallow way . . . But then, and quite different from such pleasures, and like a voice from far more distant regions . . . instantly I was uplifted into huge regions of northern sky, I desired with almost sickening intensity something never to be described . . . and then, as in the other examples, found myself at the very same moment already falling out of that desire and wishing I were back in it . . .

The quality common to the three experiences is that of an unsatisfied desire which is itself more desirable than any other satisfaction. I call it Joy, which is here a technical term and must be sharply distinguished both from Happiness and from Pleasure. Joy (in my sense) has indeed one characteristic, and one only, in common with them; the fact that anyone who has experienced it will want it again . . . (our italics)

Wallace Stevens, the American poet, in a different set of circumstances, speaks of 'a self that touches all the edges', and describes a revelatory experience, in *Notes Toward a Supreme Fiction*:

Perhaps
The truth depends on a walk around a lake,

A composing as the body tires, a stop
To see hepatica, a stop to watch
A definition growing certain and

A wait within that certainty, a rest
In the sways of pine-trees bordering the lake,
Perhaps there are times of inherent excellence,

As when the cock crows on the left and all
Is well, incalculable balances,
At which a kind of Swiss perfection comes . . .

The 'Paradise Factor', according to Paul of Tarsus, is the process by which an individual, who has been enslaved by sin in a variety of spiritually destructive practices, is delivered from that malevolent bondage by following Christ into an acceptance of death of self; and through resurrection and regeneration is raised into a new and triumphant life. The 'Paradise Factor' is being delivered from alienation from God in the kingdom of darkness, and being transformed into communion with God in the kingdom of light. The 'Paradise Factor' for Paul was the experience: ' . . . caught up to the third heaven. Whether it was in the body or out of the body I do not know—God knows. And I know that this man . . . was caught up to Paradise.'

The Psalmist describes the 'Paradise Factor':

I said to the Lord, 'You are my Lord; apart from you I have no good thing . . .

'Lord, you have assigned me my portion and my cup; you have made my lot secure. The boundary lines have fallen for me in pleasant places; surely I have a delightful inheritance . . .

'You have made known to me the path of life; you will fill me with joy in your presence, with eternal pleasures at your right hand.'

The capacity to experience the Paradise Factor is implanted in every man and woman at birth as pleasurable sensations begin to impinge on the newborn child. Depending on their environment it either increases or diminishes with experience, but memory dims as age increases and individuals distance themselves from God, and the Paradise Factor disappears through indifference or neglect. To recover that diminishing and tantalising memory men and women seek replacements for an unknown God in things which synthetically excite, titillate or stimulate—sex, sport, work, church, politics, gambling and all forms of chemical addiction. What any chemical or behavioural 'junkie' seeks in all of these activities is the 'Paradise Factor'—but they give it other names such as 'hit', 'high', 'rush', 'satisfaction', 'euphoria', 'pleasure', 'enjoyment'.

The Paradise Factor is the unique joy and despair of all addicts.

It is now officially admitted by those in authority in the superpower United States of America that the No. 1 problem facing the nation—and other Western nations as well—is addictive substance abuse. The United States, with 5 per cent of the world's population, is said to consume 50 per cent of the world's illicit supplies of cocaine. After twenty years of trying to solve the drug problem by interdicting supplies it is now openly admitted that the problem is one of American *demand*, not of foreign *supply*.

Writing in the *New York Times* (16 August, 1988), Tom Wicker said:

> Even in an age of nuclear weapons, renewed racial problems, a battered and failing environment, huge deficits and staggering poverty, polls show that Americans believe the drug traffic is the No.1 national problem . . . Admiral Carlisle Trust, the Chief of Naval Operations, said in a recent speech that the Armed Forces could not stop drug smuggling

'because the economic incentives are so potent
and the network of communications from farm
to market via thousands of boats and small
planes is so extensive' . . . Trying to combat
drugs by stopping the flow from the evil world
into this innocent country, the favoured aim of
this feckless legislation, is a hopeless task . . .

Writing in the *New York Times* (8 December, 1989), a
former Secretary of Health, Education and Welfare, Joseph
A. Califano Jr., declared:

Addiction to alcohol and drugs, legal and
illegal, crowds every nook and cranny of our
nation. Its economic costs—in health care,
crime, lost productivity, forfeited education,
property destruction—will top (US)$300
billion this year and, unchecked, reach the
trillion dollars by the mid-1990s.

Addiction in America gives new meaning to
the word awesome: 57 million Americans are
hooked on cigarettes; 18 million are addicted to
alcohol or abuse it; 21 million have tried
cocaine; more than one million are hooked on
crack; seven million smoke marijuana at least
once a week; as many as one million are
hooked on heroin; ten million abuse
tranquillisers and other psychotherapeutic
drugs; one million regularly use hallucinogens
like LSD and PCP; and ice—smokeable speed
and a likely candidate to succeed crack as the
1990s drug of the month—has already hooked
thousands.

Addiction is Public Health Enemy No.1.
Half the nation's hospital patients and most
homeless people suffer from alcohol or drug
abuse . . . A fundamental shift in society's

> culture is critical . . . what we should fear above
> all is the judgement of God and history if we,
> the most affluent people on earth, free to act as
> we choose, choose not even to try . . .

For the past twenty years international criminal organisations—Chinese triads, Sicilian and Corsican mafias, South American cartels, Cuban and Jamaican and Puerto Rican gangs—have all known that *demand* was the most important factor in drug abuse, and they gamble billions of dollars and their lives on this judgement. Their profits are in the region of US$150 billion a year.

But political leaders from all parties in all Western nations, with a consistent record of failure in dealing with the drug problem over the same period, are satisfied with spending a few million dollars unsuccessfully seeking to interdict *supplies*, and on equally unsuccessful education schemes. Ironically, the latter have been provided by doctors, psychiatrists and sociologists, who have a parallel record of failure. Further, doctors and psychiatrists not only provide drugs of abuse, they are probably the profession most addicted to abusing them—for example, the high rate of alcoholism in the medical profession.

Why are the American and other Western nations so compulsively determined to destroy their health, their families, their environment, their very existence, for the sake of an ephemeral experience?

The 'Paradise Factor' is rarely if ever mentioned in drug treatment circles, even by the experts. That is not because they have not *observed* it, but because they have not *understood* it. The reason for this is because of the associated complexity of addiction symptomatology. There was plenty of galactic evidence around the cosmos for Einstein and others to have several explanatory theories, but Einstein wanted a *unitary* theory to demonstrate that 'God does not play dice with the universe'.

The 'unitary theory' in the complex world-wide problem

of addiction is 'the Paradise Factor'. It is the fundamental reason why people of all nations and ages and religions and classes take chemicals at whatever personal risk and cost. The chemicals let them experience, psychologically and physiologically, what parents and priests and politicians never told them: Paradise is only a decision away.

Just pick up the telephone. Walk to the street corner. Ask a colleague. Visit the doctor. A chemical 'high' awaits that will take them out of one world and put them in another. Einstein's theory only required one step—and it took an individual to the moon. But it was a giant step for the one who took it.

Concerned parents can plead ruined bodies and careers, concerned priests can preach pending damnation and threatened salvation, and concerned politicians can pontificate about national values being undermined; but the individual who has discovered that, beyond a visionless society in which they struggle through a sterile existence, there is a paradise within to be entered by taking one short step, is prepared to sacrifice family and job and community and nation in search of that moon-distant Paradise Factor. That empyrean vision is what creates a relentless demand for drugs.

In the 1990s a new generation has been seeking the same 'Paradise Factor' as their predecessors of the 1960s to 1980s, because it is inherent in all men and women—especially when knowledge of the truly satisfying spiritual is withheld from them in homes, schools and most social circumstances. In his book, *Storming Heaven*, Jay Stevens records a few verbatim quotations from individuals who were experimenting with new drugs in the 1980s:

> Although still the most popular name, lately there has been a lobbying effort to discard psychedelic as irreversibly tainted by Leary, Kelsey, the hippies *et al.*, and replace it with entheogen, a bit of philology best translated as 'the god within' . . .

LSD, while still available as a street drug, was considered somewhat antiquated by the professional explorers of inner space. It has been superseded by a new generation of psychedelics with names like Ecstasy, Adam, Intellex, 2CB, Vitamin K, and a handful of others, most synthesised from various methamphetamines and tryptomines . . .

Tarcher was a staunch supporter of Ecstasy: 'Vitamin K gives a wild and imaginative trip, but it is of no transcendental meaning. Ecstasy, on the other hand, is an exquisitely useful, heart-opening, defence-destroying, insight-provoking drug, which is bound to give a help in any psychotherapeutic process' . . .

Some comments (concerning Ecstasy) were: 'They wanted to create a more spiritual substance. So they worked on it, shaving off molecules, polishing it for about fifteen years and when it finally came out people said, "This is it" . . .

'It's an empathy drug. What I've noticed about this stuff is that it eliminates the effects of the past, like fear. It's the perfect domestic psychedelic. It kind of melts defences. I have found it to be very healing and helpful. It's a very transformative experience' . . .

The most recent idea—highly publicised by prominent figures in the USA and UK—that, somehow, encouraging people to 'Just Say No', with an implicit warning that what the individual was doing was 'bad for them', was enough to put a stop to addictions, is ludicrous. It has been known for a number of years, both inside and outside the laboratory, that pain was not an adequate teaching tool, whereas pleasure was. From his experiments with rats stimulating the pleasure areas by means of implanted electrodes in the brain, B. F. Skinner, the authority on Behaviourism, said:

> The effect of punishment was a temporary
> suppression of the behaviour, not a reduction in
> the total number of responses. Even under
> severe and prolonged punishment, that rate of
> responding will rise when punishment has been
> discontinued . . . It is found that after a given
> time the rate of responding is no lower than if
> no punishment had taken place.

It was even found that punishment actually reinforced
the behaviour it was designed to obliterate.

In another series of experiments recorded by H. J.
Campbell in his book, *The Pleasure Areas*, he expands on the
importance of the pleasure principle:

> With intracranial self-stimulation both lower
> forms and people behave in a compulsive and
> exclusive fashion. They wish to do nothing
> other than the minimum requirement to obtain
> limbic stimulation, pressing the lever
> repetitively with no thought for food or drink
> or any other necessity of life. This
> compulsiveness, this exclusiveness, suggested to
> me that everything the animal does in its
> normal life, its entire behaviour, is directed at
> evoking electrical activity in the pleasure areas
> of the brain. The only reason animals do
> anything at all is to produce what could be
> obtained so easily by pressing the lever.
> Whatever else they do simply accomplishes in a
> poor degree what the lever supplies sublimely
> and exquisitely. So I have suggested the
> principle which is the axiom of my theory of
> behaviour, namely, that the pleasure areas *must*
> be activated if life is to continue; it is a built-in

> property of nervous systems, at least of the
> complexity of vertebrates, to generate
> behaviour that insures that the limbic brain
> regions are maintained in a state of electrical
> activation . . .

Campbell went on to affirm that if the stimulation was
continued without respite, as with some animals, the animal
died rejecting food and drink. Under 'natural' conditions—
that is, where the limbic areas were activated by stimulation
of peripheral receptors—this behaviour was not maintained
for long, because of a threefold neural mechanism of the
sensory system, which allowed the body to 'adapt'. This
meant that although a sense organ responded to stimulation
by generating a barrage of nerve impulses into the brain, the
receptor gradually slowed down and finally ceased to
discharge impulses even though the stimulus continued.

It has been demonstrated in the laboratory that a
monkey, once addicted to the pleasure of cocaine, will self-
administer the drug until it dies. One of them pressed a bar
12,800 *times* to obtain a single dose of cocaine. In another
series of laboratory experiments recorded by H. J. Campbell
in his book, *The Pleasure Areas*, he chose a stimulus that
could not be thought to evoke any kind of psychological
reaction (for example, he said that some monkeys would
choose landscapes instead of lamp-posts when shown slides).
He chose white light, and connected the capacitance probe
and stimulator to a high wattage bulb placed a few inches in
front of the animals' cages. The tests were carried out
without any deprivation of food or drink or sensation. The
animal stayed in its usual cage under its usual living
conditions, and the apparatus was introduced at irregular
intervals. Campbell reported:

> When the capacitance probe is first pushed
> through the bars the squirrel monkeys come
> running up to investigate it. They handle it

spontaneously in the way monkeys manipulate any new object they come across. Unless it proves edible, or can be made love to, the new object is soon tired of and ignored. But our squirrel monkeys did not tire quickly of the capacitance probe.

During the first test session they touched it about thirty times, sporadically and rather absentmindedly after the initial decision that it was neither meat nor mate. Their limbs happened to come into contact with the probe as they moved about the cage and stared at the five-hundred-watt lamp that went on and off a few inches in front of them without their understanding why . . . On about the fourth day the monkeys touched the probe some two hundred times in fifteen minutes, and within a week they reached out and grabbed the probe before it could be pushed through the bars. After that they touched the probe at a fairly steady rate of three hundred to five hundred times during a test session, with the light actually on for a total of thirteen minutes. This means they learned to release the probe and touch it again in an average of two-tenths of a second . . .

Those who advocate restraint—such as in the highly-touted officially approved 'Just Say No' campaign—are the most dangerous and negative part of the rapidly increasing drug problem. This is because they show themselves to be totally uninformed about the effects of drugs, or to be unduly dependent on so-called psychiatrist 'experts'—who have years of demonstrable failure behind them; and to the person who genuinely wishes to stop the abuse this ignorance is a major obstacle.

Even outside the confines of the laboratories it has been

found that many animals seek out plants for their stimulating effect. It is not only rats and monkeys that responded to the pleasure stimulus—cats, rabbits, guinea pigs, dogs, dolphins, goldfish all respond similarly. But only humans can describe what happens, and they are agreed that stimulation affects their moods. In some areas of stimulation drug-like euphoric feelings were generated; in other areas, it produced discomfort—such as fear, anxiety, foreboding, alienation.

In a series of studies conducted by the international authority on addictions, Dr Charles P. O'Brien, and his associates at the University of Pennsylvania School of Medicine, they discovered three important factors relating to drug addicts being conditioned by their drug-environment. First, drug-related areas are specific to each individual—what is arousing to one individual in the environment has little effect on another. Secondly, an objective physiological response did not always coincide with the addict's subjective condition. Thirdly, and most important, emotions and thought patterns played a major role in responses. If a patient used drugs to relieve fear or anxiety or depression then the mood state could later precipitate a craving. This meant that the addict had two conditions to be treated: drug craving, and mood-disorder.

Outside the laboratories, experimentation has been conducted into 'auto-conditioning training', a technique that—for example, with athletes aspiring to international honours—helps individuals to choose their moods and thoughts at will to reach their goal. This is accompanied by 'Kirlian electrobioluminescence'—the study of human aura that reveals the general level of metabolic processes in the body; if the aura seems out of order, the relevant organs are stimulated with a laser beam to achieve maximum performance.

In the Moscow National Research Institute of Physical Culture there is training in 'futuristic sports techniques' in which the nature of athletic inspiration is analysed, and it is taught there are three components: physical, emotional (moods and feelings) and mental (thoughts). When inspired, most of the athletes experience diverse physical sensations—a tingling in the lower face, coolness at the sides of the face, and a sensation of lightness in the body. Courses are taught in which these symptoms are reproduced at will by means of auto-conditioning, so that the athletes enter their event with 'optimal moods of joy, happiness or anger'. Other courses are taught in how the opposite effects might be induced in competition rivals. Acupuncture points, especially in the region of the ear, are used to evaluate the condition of different bodily systems, and if there is a 'reduced potential' it is stimulated with a laser beam.

While on the subject of athletics, it has been discovered that some athletes not only take anabolic steroids to give them an extra 'high', but some take 'oxygen cocktails'—a kind of drink enriched with glucose and vitamins filled with bubbles of pure oxygen. Since oxygen is absorbed much more slowly from the stomach than from the lungs, a treated runner has a greater supply of oxygen than his rivals.

This sensitivity to 'outside' impulses has been noted by other observers in the field of philosophy as well as medicine. Sir John Eccles, the noted neurophysiologist, discussing the relationship between the mind and the brain, described the brain as a system of 'ten thousand million neurones . . . momentarily poised close to a just-threshold level of excitability. It is the kind of machine that a "ghost" could operate if by "ghost" we mean in the first place an "agent" whose action has escaped detection even by the most delicate instruments.' Sir John Eccles believed that extrasensory perception and psychokinesis were weak and irregular manifestations of the principle which allows an individual's mental volition to influence his own material brain to give rise to conscious experiences.

The Paradise Factor is not a chemical, however, nor a stimulated sensation, but a relationship. The Paradise Factor is a clue, not a solution. Chemicals also may provide a clue, but only God provides a solution. Even glossolalia, or speaking in tongues, whether practised by Christians in churches or Tibetans in monasteries, is only an induced behavioural paradisal sensation providing a clue to a deeper relationship with God.

Ultimately, all addictions—behavioural as well as chemical—are bondages to sensation. Addiction means bondage. The sensation—the 'hit', or 'high', or 'rush', or 'ecstasy', experienced by chemical or behavioural abusers of all kinds—has been described by the more articulate as 'like being kissed by God'. The Paradise Factor.

It is not the chemical itself which is the addict's chief problem—caffeine, alcohol, nicotine, cocaine, heroin, barbiturates, amphetamines, tranquillisers—but the sensation which they induce. The slow build-up of anticipated delight, the quickened rush of pleasure, the explosion of orgasmic ecstasy, the quiet afterglow of content, the untroubled sense of self-transcendence. The Paradise Factor.

But these sensations constituting the Paradise Factor—the goal of all chemical and behavioural addicts—are also not the fundamental problem of the addict requiring cure; although once experienced they have to be at least replicated, if not replaced or surpassed. They are evidences of the body's psycho-physical potential to produce a 'spiritual' experience through the use of appropriate physical 'triggers'. Like the sexual experiences which they mirror, they are the body's God-given psycho-physical responses to a reciprocal stimulus. In the mutual expression of love this leads to a self-transcendent satisfaction and a heightened sense of union and communion; its abuse, however, in lust, leads to a self-centred satiety and a sense of alienation and guilt.

The addict in a secular humanist twentieth century, in bondage to whatever preferred chemical stimulus, and not provided by family, church or society with an adequate belief system of values to act as 'spiritual triggers' of the paradisal experience, has no other alternatives than the synthetic chemicals for what has been described by the scientists as 'the elevation in joy and euphoria' normally produced by the body's 'endorphins' under natural psycho-physical pressures.

The businessman with his uppers and downers and alcohol in the office drawer, the housewife with her tranquillisers in the medical cabinet or vodka in the refrigerator, the poor youths or rich yuppies with their heroin or hash or coke in their hidden 'stashes'—and all of them with their cigarettes—are emptying their bodies' receptors of natural chemicals and replacing them with synthetic substances for a temporary, illusory and 'extraordinary' (in the sense of 'above normal') experience of adequacy and enjoyment. The Paradise Factor.

But not only does this destroy their health, it also destroys their capacity to experience the real thing. Paradisal pleasure by chemical addiction is being forever titillated and never satisfied. It is being tantalised by visions of paradise while being tortured by pangs of hell. The hell of the addict is to know that paradise exists, and not to know the true path to the entrance and presence of God.

Without the chemically induced paradisal 'high' the addict wanders in the sterile hell of emptiness and meaninglessness of the 'normal' world. His or her chemical paradise of illusory self-transcendence is a temporary rose-garden of singing birds and falling waterfalls and music at the edge of sound where one is ephemerally 'kissed by God'. This is the explanation of the idiot grin of the wino and the vacuous smile of the junkie. The Paradise Factor.

Ultimately, whatever definition is used to describe the human phenomenon of addiction, it is generally agreed that it is bondage to a sensation. In his *Confessions of an Opium Eater*, Thomas de Quincey said: 'Happiness now may be bought for a penny, and carried in the waistcoat pocket.' This convenient, if elusive, portmanteau expression, 'happiness', is the sensation experienced by all addicts. The bitter fact that it is a chimerical, chemically-induced illusion is for the morning after; at the height of the experience of seductive stupor it is paradise regained.

This is the real problem of drug abuse. Not the criminal

mafia, or syndicates, or barons; not the dealers, or pushers, or distillers, or publicans; not uncaring governments, or incompetent psychiatrists, or uninformed sociologists; but how to replace the known illusion of happiness with the unknown real thing?

Once the paradisal pleasure of the addictive chemical has been experienced, all other normal sources of pleasure—family, friends, home, job, sport, possessions and health—fade into insignificance. The addict has been 'kissed by God', and the world is a different place. Like the animal in the laboratory, he or she knows how the body can be made to provide indescribable pleasure beyond food and sex, and they will return innumerable times to that source in a frantic search for the renewal of that experience.

But, more than the animal, the human addict has passed beyond the body's responses, beyond the restrictions of the mind's frontiers, into the vast unknown continent of the spirit, where God dwells in ineffable joy and light and love and peace. The return from that supernal realm to the 'real world'—where the paradisal supernal realm and experience is usually denied and derided by the accepted 'experts' of secularism—alienates the addict for ever from the self-appointed, non-spiritual sciolists with their limited material solutions for the complex psycho-spiritual addiction problem.

The reasons for the nationally negative social aspects of addiction which drive so many to seek paradisal relief have been listed by the noted Harvard psychiatrist, Dr Armand Nicholi, in a *New England Journal of Medicine* article entitled, 'A Modern Epidemic':

> . . . In essence people take these drugs to alter or escape from a less than tolerable society, and to meet intense emotional needs . . .
> . . . In addition, a vast body of research has shown that the absence of a parent through death, divorce, or a time-demanding job, contributes to many forms of emotional

disorder, especially the anger, rebelliousness, low self-esteem, depression and anti-social behaviour that characterises drug abusers. Changes in child-rearing practices and family stability in the United States, beginning several years before the drug culture evolved, have shifted child care from parents to other agencies . . . American parents spend less time with their children than parents in any other nation of the world except England. The accelerating divorce rate in the United States has closely paralleled the rise in drug use, and over half the children under the age of 18 (approximately 13 million) live in a home with one or both parents missing . . .

Why does America have a greater drug problem than any other country? Because what they were led to believe in home and school and college and church as 'God's own country' turned out to be a spiritual lie but a chemical truth. Paradise for addicts was not to be found even in a church—other than a few exceptions—but it could be discovered in a pill or a powder or a bottle.

And what do the country's political and ecclesiastical leaders offer as a solution to the national demand for paradisal experience? An hour of confession in a self-help group? A meal in a soup kitchen? A sermon about 'a Power out there'? A rebuke about a wasted life? A glib—and failed—psychiatric theory? Methadone or Naltrexone or Clonidine or Desipramine? A 'Just Say No' campaign?

'Just Say No' to Paradise? 'Just Say No' to being kissed by God? Are the people who dream up these campaigns mad, or ignorant, or blind, or venal? In 'God's own country', whose motto is 'In God We Trust', where major political battles are fought over the issue of prayer in schools, where almost half the population believe in the possibility of being born again by resurrection power, do these leaders really expect the chemically-addicted two-thirds of the nation to live a negative existence that excludes the possibility of a paradise experience on earth? Do they themselves 'Just Say No' to all forms of chemical substances—or behavioural addictions?

The most important question of all at this time of international addiction crisis is: where are the Christian church's spiritual leaders clearly articulating spiritual solutions to their respective national spiritual problems?

A report in the *Sunday Times* (24 December, 1989) revealed the findings of an opinion poll that 74 per cent of Britain's population believed in God, 70 per cent believed in Jesus as Son of God, but that the Church came *third*—behind parents and schools—as a body setting the nation's spiritual standards. Only one person in five went to church at Christmas, Easter and for special services; and only 15 per cent went to church once or more. The institutional Christian church in Britain is out of touch with, and has no significant message for, the society it is supposed to influence paradisally for Jesus Christ.

Addiction, says God, began in the paradisal Garden of Eden. For if the positive experience of addiction is paradise, the negative experience is bondage. Addiction means bondage. We were all—men and women—created to be addicted to God. Outside that divine addiction in a beneficent paradise there are only personal individual hells of tantalising and transient illusion.

The story of the Garden of Eden is of a Paradise where God's creatures, made in God's own image, were created with a *contingent* freedom. They were free, said God, to eat of everything—except the tree of the knowledge of good and evil. They were stewards of God in a Garden where there was no decay, and they were given dominion over an animal world where there was no death—so long as they remembered they were addicted to God's service and purpose.

It was their misconception of human freedom, the creaturely responsibilities of spiritual addiction to their Creator, which tore them from Paradise and subjected them to godless exile from the presence of God. They construed their *contingent* freedom as *absolute* freedom, hungered illicitly for the forbidden knowledge of evil, and were left with only faint memories of Paradise lost. The Garden of Eden was where what Alcoholics Anonymous describes as 'self-will-run-riot'—that fundamental symptom of all addicts—happened the first time. When Adam and Eve took of the fruit of the tree of knowledge of good and evil they became the world's first junkies. They chose the self-will orgasmic junk of the illusory transcendent high promised them by Satan—'You shall be as gods knowing good and evil'—rather than the undiluted joy of an addicted union with God.

Paradise was walking and talking guilt-free with God. Paradise was enjoying each other and God's creation without fear. Paradise was having everything except a knowledge of evil. Paradise was transcendence over every created thing as addicted stewards of God. Paradise was the ecstasy of knowing that they were God's chosen to walk and talk and fulfil a divine purpose on earth together. Paradise was where they were kissed by God every day. Paradise was where joy reigned unconfined so long as human creatures accepted their contingent freedom, their fundamental addiction to God. Rejecting contingent freedom for the myth of god-like absolute freedom, they and their descendants are condemned to live outside Paradise, haunted by atavistic memories of what they know exists beyond the flaming sword-bearing cherubim. Having been kissed by God they know the world has no comparable satisfactions. They are tormented by 'the Paradise Factor'—the pursuit of happiness in chemicals or ritualistic behaviour.

It is this atavistic response that has created the demand for chemical stimulants at the expense of all other relationships, at least since the time that Noah got drunk on his own home-grown wine and brought a curse on his son, Canaan. It is the *demand* for chemical stimulants which causes 'the drug problem', and not the *supply*. If the supply had ever been a problem God would have dealt with it at the had ever been a problem God would have dealt with it at the source, by eliminating the cause, or by direct command forbidding use. Instead God only provided warnings regarding abuse, and left the responsibility for regulating this to each individual.

Yet governments persist in policies of throwing money futilely on risible law enforcement measures, in ignorance or defiance of historical experience. They stubbornly refuse to acknowledge the obvious failure of such policies of interdiction of supply wherever practised, and refuse to address themselves to the obvious cause of the drug problem in the public demand for chemical substances. All current policies have failed in western countries, for it is officially acknowledged internationally by all investigating bodies that addiction is 'the world's worst social problem'.

In his important article in the New York Times already quoted (pp. 25–26) Joseph A. Califano asserts:

> For the nation's (US)$300 billion problem, the Government is only investing $500 million in all research on addiction. This includes the hunt for heroin substitutes less debilitating than methadone and new drugs to reduce the craving for cocaine and crack; finding ways to quit smoking and avoid using prescription drugs; understanding alcoholism and the genetics and psychology of addiction; and developing prevention and treatment programmes . . .
>
> Since 1980 the Government has spent $2.2 trillion on defence. Over that same period it has spent $21 billion for its various wars on drugs. In all five years of World War II we suffered fewer than 300,000 battlefield deaths. Each year the death toll of alcoholism, drug abuse and addiction is almost twice that number . . .
>
> What we should fear above all is the judgement

> on earth, free to act as we choose, choose not even
> to try . . . (our italics)

Criminals have a greater knowledge of this human condition than politicians, physicians, psychiatrists, priests, pastors, police or media pundits. Every day Asian, European, North and South American members of criminal organisations risk their money, their freedom and their lives on the basis of a conviction that men and women everywhere in the world will pay a high price—in every sense of that term—for a chemical giving a momentary experience of pleasure. The Paradise Factor. They make profits of some US$150 *billion* a year backing their judgement of people against that of the pathetic platitudes of politicians, psychiatrists and parents advocating 'Just Say No', or 'Do Without Today'. The contempt of the criminals for such is exceeded only by the contempt of the addict who has been 'kissed by God'.

CHAPTER 2

Lessons from the Past

Two of the most successful procedures in the treatment of hard drug addictions in recent years have been privately initiated projects: the now-defunct Synanon, based in California; and the Minnesota Method, based in Minnesota. Synanon was the creation of an ex-alcoholic member of Alcoholics Anonymous, Charles 'Chuck' Dederich; and the Minnesota Method was the creation of a multidisciplinary team dissatisfied with existing addiction treatment systems.

The Synanon programme, although now discredited because of the egotistical excesses of its founder (to curtail criticism he had a rattlesnake dropped into the letterbox of a lawyer who was trying to get a patient out of the pro- gramme), is currently being widely used under different names in several national and international treatment organisations. (George, with his BBC television colleague, Norman Stone, made the only television documentary about Synanon, as all other news organisations backed away from the subject because of the huge litigation suits launched against them by Dederich.)

Synanon was the personal brainchild of Chuck Dederich, and was created by him because of what he felt were the inadequacies of Alcoholics Anonymous. Beginning in a small drug treatment unit in Santa Monica, California, he and a few colleagues built up a USA-wide organisation of successful and widely publicised treatment centres. The Synanon method was based solely on the empirical reading and practices of Chuck

Dederich. He borrowed ideas from Thomas Aquinas, Ralph Waldo Emerson, Ernest Fromm, and whichever author he was currently reading. These were tested in a central practice known as 'the Synanon Game', in which addicts supervised by counsellors participated in a targeted and savagely orchestrated encounter experience. In 'the Game', as members confessed their experiences, the confession-member was subjected to sustained criticism, and systematically stripped bare of all hypocritical pretences in his or her confession. In addition to the confessed experiences, the known past or present conduct of the individual was subjected to intense scrutiny and bombardment, until he or she broke—when the emphasis shifted to another targeted individual.

The encounter therapy was restricted to the time-frame of 'the Game' only. When 'the Game' finished at the discretion of the presiding counsellor, nothing of what had been confessed or challenged or alleged was permitted to be mentioned, except between the individual and the counsellor. From the moment 'the Game' ended the treatment emphasis was shifted to one of conspicuous compassionate and understanding support by all Synanon members and counsellors.

This central experience was coordinated with a structured programme of skills training in the Synanon community. This included everything from working in the Synanon bakery, building, printing, farming, crafts, photography and painting, etc. to participating in local community work projects. The surplus products from the Synanon projects were sold by members in the locality, then the state, and finally across the nation. This meant developing expertise in management, marketing, distribution, organisation and a number of related skills.

Within a period of ten years, in the 1970s, Synanon grew from being just a drug treatment unit to being 'Synanon City', 'Synanon Nationwide', and 'Synanon Religion'. When the BBC television documentary was filmed in 1981 Synanon was planning to set up international representation. Its success was phenomenal—and the failures obscured by its rapid expansion. From successfully treating drug addicts only in the early 1970s, Synanon expanded into treating 'addictions' of a more general nature among the Californian community at large. At one time it was estimated that over four thousand non-resident people were meeting regularly every weekend at Synanon in San Francisco for 'a spiritually transforming experience'.

The organiser of this 'experience', Terry Hurst, had first gone to Synanon with her drug-addict husband. He had been successfully treated and had risen to become President of the Synanon Foundation. Terry Hurst told us that Synanon was the ideal community of her dreams, and that of everyone who joined the community. Her created 'spiritual experience' programme, in association with Dederich, for the visiting weekenders was: 24 hours of fasting; then an 'exquisite, orchestrated experience' of gourmet food and wines in an ambience of beautiful music for 24 hours. The final 24 hours included participation in the confrontational 'Synanon Game' for several hours, culminating in 'warm and loving fellowship with the other members of the regular Synanon community'.

But the strictly authoritarian regime of Chuck Dederich rapidly progressed into self-imposed tyranny. 'He wasn't the only mind in Synanon,' Terry Hurst said, 'nor had he the only thoughts regarding development; but until he approved a proposal it just wasn't done.' Instead of constructive theories from his reading, his programme began to incorporate bizarre personal ideas. He introduced mass divorces, mass marriages, wife swapping, and eventually mass vasectomies. His 'health groups' became karate-trained 'goon squads', carrying weapons to keep out the increasing number of investigators, media, lawyers and anxious families.

Terry Hurst, who had to flee and hide herself because she chose to confront Chuck Dederich at one staff 'Game' session, admitted that, had Dederich not developed his megalomania she would gladly have stayed with the Synanon programme. 'It changed my life,' she said, 'and it changed the lives of all those who experienced it. The central emphasis of Synanon was on this capacity to change; and that individuals, no matter how bad, could be changed into different and better persons. Change of personality was fundamental, and there was a driving sense of purpose as the whole community was motivated towards this end.'

However, Terry Hurst also conceded that the Synanon programme was only successful so long as individuals stayed within the Synanon community. Once they left to take up normal living outside the Synanon community they went back on to drugs, alcohol and the old life. Chuck Dederich himself, she said, eventually returned to drugs and alcohol.

But many of the treatment theories that were first developed by Synanon are now the basic practices of leading drug and alcohol abuse treatment centres in the United States and Europe—unattributed, of course, after Synanon's fall from grace.

The other successful chemical substance abuse treatment programme to emerge in recent years is the Minnesota Method. It also arose out of Alcoholics Anonymous. But it diverged in a number of critical ways from both Alcoholics Anonymous and Synanon, and with more limited success.

The 'Minnesota Experience'—as it was called by Dr Daniel J. Anderson, one of the leading pioneers of what later came to be termed the Minnesota Method—arose out of despair at the failures of all the other methods of alcoholism treatment in the 1950s. He was part of a team at Willmar State Hospital treating alcoholics with little success, and he set out to devise a new approach to treatment.

Their first breakaway from orthodoxy began with the theory that 'alcoholism is an illness', because of the behavioural and pathological aspects of the condition. They then decided that 'alcoholism is a no-fault illness', because— if the hypothesis was correct that it was an illness—it followed that the alcoholic could not be held personally responsible for the condition. Because alcoholism and drug addiction were both generally viewed as 'inebriety', it was only a short step to including other forms of chemical abuse within their treatment hypothesis and programme.

These basic assumptions led to other treatment theories. Since, in their postulated view, there was no hope of finding any underlying cause of alcoholism (and other addictions) they decided to focus on *caring* rather than *curing*. In the words of Dr Anderson:

'We accepted the fact that we would not be able to get at predisposing causes of the condition and root them out. We knew that we would not be able to cure the alcoholic; in fact, that concept had a long history of failure . . . This then became our goal: to help the alcoholic learn to live with and cope with this chronic condition.'

Although there has been considerable favourable publicity in the popular media regarding the Minnesota Method, the independently published figures do not support the optimistic claims made on its behalf. In a recent study published in the *British Journal of Addiction* (1988, 83, 735–748) entitled: 'The Minnesota Method in the Management of Drug and Alcohol Dependency: miracle, method or myth', by Christopher C. H. Cook, he stated:

> Despite extravagant claims of success, there appear to be few follow-up studies of patients graduating from Minnesota-type programmes . . . Rossi, Stach & Bradley (1963) published a more detailed study about five years after the first follow-up in 1955, and the authors suggest that it shows no appreciable change in effectiveness of their programme over this period . . . while these studies show valuable and impressive results, they are methodologically deficient. No account was taken of any other treatments obtained by patients between discharge and follow-up. No control or comparison group of patients was included . . .

Alongside their restricted and negative treatment process, however, they discovered a new positive factor. Derived from the experience with Alcoholics Anonymous they found that one of the most powerful therapeutic effects on their patients did not come from their professional staff, but from the interaction of patients with recovered alcoholic counsellors in small, task-oriented discussion groups. In these groups the subjects of most help were those relating to 'resentment, denial, blame and grandiosity'. They also discovered that 'the helper seems to get as much help as the person being helped'.

Despite the theoretically-imposed limitations of the Minnesota Method, the pioneers concluded that the help of a clergyman was necessary for certain 'steps'; that the person had to admit to personal powerlessness, that he or she had 'a crucial need to change their behaviour', and that they had an ability to make that change.

Christopher C. H. Cook, in the article quoted above, also recorded a research study—conducted by proponents of the Minnesota Method on 'self-reports' from 482 patients at nearby Hazeldon—who declared the benefits of the treatment in their own words, as follows:

> . . . The most salient findings were that (i) the most important events involved the daily lectures with resultant insight, (ii) one-to-one conferences with staff members were also reported as significant and meaningful, (iii) visitors, telephone calls and mail were frequently reported by patients as meaningful, and (iv) for many patients a return to previously acquired religious beliefs or an awakening interest in spirituality was a profound enough experience for them to comment about it frequently.

So, while Synanon had a rationalistic treatment

programme for change based on empirical literary theories, the Minnesota Method had a hybrid-spiritual treatment programme based on Alcoholics Anonymous' 'Twelve Steps'. Synanon believed in caring for and curing the addicts; the Minnesota Method believes in caring for but not curing them.

Of these two leading treatment programmes, now being used with variations throughout the world, Synanon alone addressed itself to the 'transcendence factor' of addictions. All other programmes address the negative, getting rid of 'the monkey-on-the-back' syndrome. They either ignore, or are unaware of, the significant part played by the paradisal experience of the chemical abuser and the inherent necessity to replicate, replace or enhance it.

Teaching the alcoholic or addict to 'cope with', or 'live with', their condition 'one day at a time' is the easiest part of any treatment programme. Providing an alternative to the paradisal experience the alcoholic or addict has known when on their chemical of abuse is a much more difficult matter altogether. It requires personal experience of the spiritual nature of the Paradise Factor, something that is not taught in medical, nursing, sociology or psychology classes—unless in a negative sense. That is why it is ignored, or never attempted by the Freudian, Jungian or Behaviourist psychiatrists dominating the field of addictions.

It is comparatively easy to devise a programme to help an alcoholic to pass a bar, a gambler to pass a betting shop, a workaholic to restrict himself to a nine-to-five routine, and an addict to say 'No' to a pusher. It is much more difficult to provide a means whereby they can know a real and permanent transcendental experience instead of a synthetic and transient chemically or behaviourally induced one.

In China, the Marxist-Leninist late Chairman of the Chinese Communist Party, Mao Zedong, was able to change the thinking and practices of one billion people by a simple and fundamental process. Leading Western scholars of the Chinese Revolution over the past forty years have commented how Mao 'spiritually transformed' the Chinese people in two decades by 'an unique concept of revolution as a restructuring of thought rather than just the capturing of state power'.

The politics and ethics of the Mao process are discussed in George's book[1]; it is the efficacy of the process as a means of change that interests us here. Mao's theory of change for individuals and nations was based on the fundamental two-fold proposition:

(i)   the human mind is infinitely malleable, and able to expand spiritually;
(ii) the human will, once rectified, is all-powerful, to the point that 'the subjective creates the objective'.

From this foundation the 'process of change' was encapsulated in a three-stage process:

(i)   *mould* the human mind;
(ii) *expand* its spirituality;
(iii) *harness* its latent subjective power to create the necessary objective changes.

This was accomplished by another three-stage process:

(i)   *struggle* between old practices to be jettisoned and new concepts to be acquired;
(ii) *criticism* of ingrained and destructive traditions and superstitions;
(iii) *transformation* into dynamic new 'spiritual' men and women.

So, change in individuals is possible and attainable by mechanistic and rational means. China has no alcohol problem and, so far as is known, no recent national opium or

1. *The China Paradox: Christ versus Marx* (Milton Keynes: Nelson Word, 1990)

heroin problem after centuries of abuse. It has, however, probably the world's worst nicotine problem. What is of interest to us here is that Mao was able to devise a process of radical change of individuals within Marxism.

It is even more possible to devise a better means of change based on Judaeo-Christian principles.

The starting point of cure for all forms of addiction is the absolute necessity to do something about the addicts' condition of 'emptiness and meaninglessness'. One of the world's most famous addicts is the well-known playwright, Jean Cocteau, who wrote a revealing book out of his own experiences as an addict *Opium: The Diary of an Addict*, in which he described his harrowing attempts to come off the drug and the doctors' attempts to cure him:

> Incredible phenomena are attached to the cure; medicine is powerless against them, beyond making the padded cell look like a hotel-room and demanding of the doctor or nurse patience, attendance and sensitivity . . .
>
> I therefore became an opium addict again because the doctors who cure—one should really say, quite simply, who purge—do not seek to cure the troubles which first cause the addiction . . .
>
> After the cure. The worst moment, the worst danger. Health with this void and an immense sadness. The doctors honestly hand you over to suicide.
>
> Now that I am cured, I feel empty, poor, heart-broken and ill . . .

The noted theologian Paul Tillich has defined *emptiness* and *meaninglessness* as the two levels of a threatening experience of non-being which attack spiritual affirmation—emptiness being the relative threat, and meaninglessness being the absolute threat. The anxiety of meaninglessness is 'anxiety about the loss of an ultimate concern of a meaning which gives meaning to all meaning'. This anxiety is aroused by the loss of a spiritual centre or locus and by a conscious lack of knowledge of the meaning of life. The loss of a spiritual centre, which leads to a loss of the meaning of life, Tillich maintains in *The Courage To Be*, follows the loss of God in the lives of individuals:

> . . . The decisive event which underlies the search for meaning and despair of it in the twentieth century is the loss of God in the nineteenth century. Feuerbach explained God away in terms of the infinite desire of the human heart; Marx explained him away in terms of an ideological attempt to rise above the given reality; Nietzche as a weakening of the will to live. The result is the pronouncement, 'God is dead', and with him the whole system in which one lived.

Dr Carl Jung, in his psychology, is essentially concerned with the search for wholeness, bringing together all the individual's characteristics—good and evil, conscious and unconscious—into the conscious experience of completeness and awareness. In *Modern Man in Search of a Soul*, he demonstrated that the most advanced thinking supports the conviction that religion is a vitally necessary element in human life, delivering the human spirit from its bondage to a sterile materialism and a meaningless humanism:

> During the past thirty years people from all over the civilised countries on earth have consulted me . . . Among all my patients in the second half of life—that is to say, over thirty-five—there has not been one whose problem in the last resort was not that of finding a religious outlook on life. It is safe to say that every one

of them felt ill because he had lost that which
the living religions of every age have given to
their followers, and none of them has been
really healed who did not regain his religious
outlook ...

Jung saw men and women as possessing four basic
faculties: sensation, thinking, feeling and intuition. Some
people have more of one than another, but every one needed
a balance of four 'faculties' to be a healthy human being. The
four faculties corresponded to the obvious means by which
consciousness obtains its orientation to experience.

Jung defined the four faculties as: *sensation* (or sense
perception), which informs us that something exists; *thinking*,
which tells us what it is; *feeling*, which tells us whether it is
agreeable or not; and *intuition*, which tells us where it comes
from and where it is going. When those four basic faculties
are not in proper balance, 'disorders' occur, and these deliver
the individual concerned into doubt and uncertainty—the
twin pillars that reinforce anxiety, stress and drugs.

But it was Dr Viktor Frankl—President of the Austrian
Medical School of Psychotherapy, and Professor of Psychiatry
and Neurology at the University of Vienna—who devised the
new and effective 'third school of psychotherapy' (as distinct
from the Freudian 'will-to-pleasure', and the Adlerian 'will-to-
power') and called his treatment system 'logotherapy' (from
the Greek word *logos*, or 'meaning') with its emphasis on 'will-
to-meaning'. Frankl contended that 'being human means
being conscious and being responsible', and that an effective
therapy had to involve the basic characteristic of the 'will-to-
meaning' in individuals. He specified the 'characteristic
features of healthy human existence', as follows: (i) education
in responsibility; (ii) education in freedom to decide; and (iii)
education in spirituality. The three characteristics, he argued,
are necessary to combat emptiness and meaninglessness.

Dr Frankl emphasised that in using logotherapy it was
essential that the therapist should be neither a teacher nor a

preacher. If he or she had a personal belief system it was for that individual alone, and for the individual who asked about it. Changing the metaphor, the logotherapist was not a painter but an eye specialist; a painter paints the world as he or she sees it, but the eye specialist enables the individual to see the world as it is.

The 'world as it is' is not simply an expression of one's self; nor is it a vehicle or instrument to give one's self significance or meaning. The world is the place, or the combination of circumstances and experiences, within which one aspect of human existence and meaning is to be found; the other aspect is found within men and women who live in that world, in their own psyche and the realm of the spirit.

Frankl spent two and a half years in four different concentration camps, out of which experience he developed his 'logotherapy', and he declared in *The Doctor and the Soul*:

> We needed to stop asking about the meaning of life, and instead to think of ourselves as those who were being questioned by life—daily and hourly. Our answers must consist, not in talk and meditation, but in right action and right conduct. Life ultimately means taking the responsibility to find the right answers to its problems and to fulfil the tasks which it constantly sets for each individual.

That is why so-called 'self-actualisation' will never succeed in providing satisfaction or meaning; it is only half the solution. In self-actualisation theories, the natural tendency is for the 'normal' to become the 'ideal', since to be normal means to become oneself, to realise one's true worth, and this cannot be less than the self-creating of happiness. Setting 'self-fulfilment' as the goal of striving, and euphoria as the goal of life, the 'happiest' people are said to be those who have realised their self-conceived potentialities. They then find that the pursuit of a 'tensionless' existence—like the pursuit of happiness—turns out to be an impossible goal.

One of the leading proponents of self-actualisation, Erich Fromm, has written in *The Art of Loving*:

> Pleasure cannot be a criterion of value since some people derive pleasure from submission and not from freedom . . . from hate and not from love, from exploitation and not from productive work . . . Productiveness is man's ability to use his powers to realise the potentialities inherent in him. If we say he must use his powers, we imply that he must be free and not dependent on someone else who controls his powers. We imply, furthermore, that he is guided by reason . . . that he knows what they are, how to use them, and what to use them for. Productiveness means that he experiences himself as the embodiment of his powers as the 'actor'; that he feels himself one with his powers . . . and they are not masked from him.

The full solution, the Judaeo-Christian Scriptures assert, lies in 'self-transcendence', of which self-actualisation is but the side-effect. The Paradise Factor.

How this 'self-transcendence' operated was explained by Jesus in a process that had certain similarity with Mao's, but far exceeded Mao's in scope and content:

(i)   all men and women had alienated themselves from 'the mind of God'—the source of all fulfilment and meaning—by an arrogant exercise of self-will;

(ii) this self-will, with all its related evils, has to be recognised, confessed—to God, not to men—and repented;

(iii) this confessing of sins elicits the forgiveness,

love and power of God in making men and women 'new'.

With this as a necessary spiritual foundation for 'self-transcendence', Jesus went on to declare the paradisal rewards prepared by His Father in heaven for those who exercised their 'will-to-meaning' in choosing them:

> Blessed are the poor in spirit,
>   for theirs is the kingdom of heaven.
> Blessed are those who mourn,
>   for they will be comforted.
> Blessed are the meek,
>   for they will inherit the earth.
> Blessed are those who hunger and thirst for
>   righteousness,
>   for they will be filled.
> Blessed are the merciful,
>   for they will be shown mercy.
> Blessed are the pure in heart,
>   for they will see God.
> Blessed are the peacemakers,
>   for they will be called the sons of God.
> Blessed are those who are persecuted because
>   of righteousness,
>   for theirs is the kingdom of heaven.

What this goal and pursuit adds up to is an elimination of self—or, rather, the 'death of the old self', and its replacement by the 'new self' through Christ-implanted power. The Apostle Paul described it:

> I do not understand what I do. For what I want
> to do I do not do, but what I hate to do
> . . . It is no longer I myself who do it, but it is
> sin living in me . . . I have the desire to do what
> is good, but I cannot carry it out. For what I do

is not the good I want to do; no, the evil I do not want to do—this I keep doing. Now if I do what I do not want to do, it is no longer I who do it, but it is sin living in me that does it.

But Paul found an answer to this all-encompassing human dilemma:

I have been crucified with Christ and I no longer live, but Christ lives in me. The life I live in the body, I live by faith in the Son of God, who loved me and gave himself for me . . .

Since, then, you have been raised with Christ, set your hearts on things above, where Christ is seated at the right hand of God. Set your minds on things above, not on earthly things. For you died, and your life is now hidden with Christ in God . . .

Writing to the Roman church Paul outlined the transformation process in its simplest form:

The word is near you; it is in your mouth and in your heart, that is, the word of faith we are proclaiming. If you confess with your mouth, 'Jesus is Lord', and believe in your heart that God has raised him from the dead, you will be saved [from the daily negative experiences of defeat and sin and death, by means of] the same power that brought again Jesus Christ from the dead[2].

The Paradise Factor.

---

2. See *The Power Factor*, by the authors (Milton Keynes: Nelson Word, 1987)

CHAPTER 3

First Steps
to
Transcendence

*A*ll men and women were created to reflect the nature of God, to inhabit the presence of God, and to be like God. That is both the glory and despair of humankind. Made from dust and returning to dust, they live with a consciousness that this earth is not their true home. Whatever their philosophy, and whatever their religion, there is an expectation, a conviction, of otherness, of bliss, of nirvana, of paradise, just within reach.

Viktor Frankl, in his *Will to Meaning*, says:

> The religious man experiences his existence not only as a concrete task but as a personal mission which is given to him by a personal Being. Thus he sees his task transparently, namely, *in the light of Transcendence*; he alone can in spite of all say 'yes' to life under all conditions and circumstances—in spite of all; in spite of distress and death. (our italics)

Frankl was faced with the utter meaninglessness of life when he, with millions of his fellow-Jews, was in Auschwitz facing the ultimate horror of the holocaust of the gas chambers. Then, when out of this monumental human evil he had developed his noetic, or 'spiritual' theory of meaning in 'logotherapy', the manuscript on the subject he had so secretly and laboriously written was taken from him, he described his reaction:

> It did not even seem possible, let alone probable, that the manuscript of my first book which I had hidden in my coat when I arrived at Auschwitz would ever be rescued. Thus I had to undergo and overcome the loss of my spiritual child. And now it seemed as if nothing and no one would survive me; neither a physical nor spiritual child of my own! So I found myself confronted with the question whether under such circumstances my life was ultimately void of any meaning.
>
> Not yet did I notice that an answer to this question with which I was wrestling so passionately was already in store for me, and that soon thereafter this answer should be given to me. This was the case when I had to surrender my clothes and in turn inherited the worn-out rags of an inmate who had been sent to the gas chambers immediately after his arrival at the Auschwitz railway station. Instead of the many pages of my manuscript, I found in the pocket of my newly acquired coat a single page torn out of a Hebrew prayer book, which contained the main Jewish prayer, *Shema Ysrael*. How should I have interpreted such a 'coincidence' other than as a challenge to *live* my thoughts instead of merely putting them down on paper?

It was in these extreme circumstances that Frankl's 'third school of psychotherapy' was forged and given life—the conviction that 'the basis of neurotic existence is in a deficiency of the patient's relationship to transcendence'.

The Judaeo-Christian Scriptures categorically state:

> God created man in his own image, in the
> image of God he created him; male and female
> he created them . . . And the Lord God formed
> man from the dust of the ground and breathed
> into his nostrils the breath of life . . .

From dust to dust, and every man and woman who dies is
a silent epitaph to a God who not only says He made man
from the dust of the ground but that He will transform that
same creature from the dust of death to be like Him and to
live with Him eternally and paradisally in the heavens. As
the Apostle Paul wrote:

> Our citizenship is in heaven. And we eagerly
> await a Saviour from there, the Lord Jesus
> Christ, who, *by the power that enables him to*
> *bring everything under his control, will transform*
> *our lowly bodies so that they will be like his glorious*
> *body.* (our italics)

The ultimate Paradise Factor.

But, to be worthy of this glorious inheritance, God said
that the creatures He had made were 'to be holy as the Lord
God is holy'; and the command of Jesus to His followers was,
'Be perfect as your Father in heaven is perfect.'
Transcendence over sin and circumstances was not only a
goal for God's creatures, it was a birthright. But how that was
to be obtained was never said to be easy. 'You shall seek me
and find me, when you seek me *with all your heart,*' God
declared on one occasion. And again: 'My thoughts are not
your thoughts, neither are your ways my ways. For as the
heavens are higher than the earth, so are my ways higher
than your ways, and my thoughts than your thoughts.'

It was Sir James Jeans who conceived of thought as the
ultimate behind the order of matter itself, making the

meaning behind things lie in the ultimate pure thought behind them so that the pure thought not seen is at least as real as the matter perceived. He said:

> If the universe is a universe of thought, then its creation must have been an act of thought . . . The universe begins to look more like a great thought than a great machine. Mind no longer appears as an accidental intruder into the realm of matter; we are beginning to suspect that we ought rather to hail it as the creator and governor of the realm of matter . . . We discover that the universe shows evidence of a designing and controlling power that has something in common with our own minds . . . [with] . . . the tendency to think in the way which, for want of a better word, we describe as mathematical . . . We are not so much intruders in the universe as at first thought . . .

So, as we look outward at the vastness of the universe, downward at the first chapters of Genesis, and inward at our turbulent minds, we are as aware as Adam was on that first morning of Creation that we have been made in the image of God, to fulfil some hidden divine purpose which involves all the infinite capacities with which we have been consciously endowed. We are not only capable of walking with God, we are also able to talk with Him and enjoy every paradisal gift created by God for our enjoyment.

Paradisal joy is the divinely gifted inheritance for every creature. Solomon the Wise declared:

> Then I realised that it is good and proper for a man to eat and drink, and to find satisfaction in his toilsome labour under the sun during the few days of life God has given him—for this is

his lot. Moreover, when God gives any man
wealth and possessions, *and enables him to enjoy
them*, to accept his lot and be happy in his
work—this is a gift of God. He seldom reflects
on the days of his life, because God keeps him
occupied with gladness of heart. (our italics)

Solomon also gave the other side of that observation
when God withheld the capacity for enjoyment—the
experience of meaninglessness:

I have seen another evil under the sun, and it
weighs heavily on men. God gives a man
wealth, possessions and honour, so that he lacks
nothing his heart desires, *but God does not
enable him to enjoy them*, and a stranger enjoys
them instead. This is meaningless, a grievous
evil. (our italics)

The crux of the creative acts of God is the spoken word
of God: 'And God said . . . ', followed by its corollary, ' . . .
and it was so'. It was a common Semitic belief that there was
an intrinsic efficacy in the spoken word, that 'word' and
'deed' are the same, or should be. This was incorporated in
the Judaic, and later Christian, use of the word *logos*, meaning
'word', 'thought' and 'meaning'.

To the Jews *logos* was not merely a sound, but a dynamic
force, the *Word* of God by which He created the world and
everything in it; the very idea of the action of God, the
creative and illuminating power of God enabling the object
of His interest to accomplish His purpose. To the Greeks
logos was the *reason* of God, the principle of order under
which the universe continued to exist; it was a purpose, a
design, a plan, the mind of God controlling the world and
every man and woman in it.

It was, and is, through 'words' that God bridges the gap
between the Creator and creature, making him or her an

instrument of His purposes; just as it is 'information' which bridges the synapse between neurons, activating them into a willed response. But if that were all, then we would only be 'mirrors', and not 'images' of God, pale reflections of divine tyranny. What makes the Scripturally-revealed conception unique is the free two-way interchange of communication, where the creature can respond to the commands of God or to the promptings of His mind.

In his 'study of human nature', *The Varieties of Religious Experience*, the physician-psychologist-philosopher, William James, investigated the infinitely complex human mind and some forms of consciousness in relation to religious experience. He concluded that our normal waking consciousness, or rational consciousness, is but one special type of consciousness. All around this consciousness, and parted from it by only the flimsiest of screens, there lie potential forms of consciousness entirely different. We may go through life without suspecting their existence, but once the requisite stimulus is applied they are there in all their completeness. He continued:

> We cannot, I think, avoid the conclusion that in religion we have a department of human nature with unusually close relations to the transmarginal or subliminal region. If the word 'subliminal' is offensive to any of you . . . call the full sunlit consciousness the A-region, and call the other the B-region. The B-region, then, is obviously the larger part of each of us, for it is the abode of everything that passes as unrecorded or unobserved. It contains, for example, such things as all our momentarily inactive memories, and it harbours the springs of all our obscurely motivated passions, impulses, dislikes, likes and prejudices. Our intuitions, hypotheses, fancies, superstitions, persuasions, convictions, and in general all our

non-rational operations, come from it. It is the
source of our dreams, and apparently they may
return to it. In it arise whatever mystical
experiences we may have . . . It is also the
fountainhead of much that feeds our religion.
In persons deep in religion . . . the door into
this region seems unusually wide open . . .

Thus, we may take it that all our conscious and
unconscious material, and our spiritual experiences, are
recorded and stored by the mind, to be brought to the surface
when stimulated or challenged by some external impulse or
event.

The mind, however, is not just like an analog computer;
it is also like a radio receiver. Depending on the particular
wave-band, it can 'tune in' to a variety of experiences that
appear to exist, sight unseen, simultaneously. The 'forms' of
consciousness described by William James and others, while
discontinuous with ordinary consciousness, can determine
attitudes when called upon to do so in support of some
decision, but cannot of themselves provide guidance to
solutions—such as different radio stations or television
channels.

'They may determine attitudes,' said William James,
'though they cannot furnish formulas; and open a region
though they fail to give a map.'

The foregoing lengthy exploration of the mind's
potential is necessary for any study of addictions, because
addiction is a psycho-spiritual problem. Among their
symptoms the addicts cannot deal with people or
circumstances in their immediate environment, because of
their personal inadequacy. As the philosopher said: *adequatio
rei et intellectus* ('the understanding of the knower must be
adequate to the thing to be known'). This, in everyday
terms, means the ability of the individual must be equal to
the task of coping with family, school, office, workshop,
boardroom, household or social occasion—without the

'support' of some chemical substance. When the addict to whatever substance is deprived of this chemical support he or she soon manifests the most anti-social conduct, cogently described by one noted authority:

> Addicted patients are asocial, inadequate, immature and unstable. They are selfish and self-centred, without interest in the welfare of others, and are only concerned with their own problems. Their major problem is in their maintenance of the supply of drugs or the immediate gratification of their desire for drugs. They will resort to any means—however unreasonable or dangerous—to satisfy this insistent craving. They have failed to develop normal human relationships and are almost totally without concern for the distress they inflict on their relatives. They lack self-discipline, will-power or ambition, and avoid responsibility. They have a low threshold for pain or any form of discomfort, and are unable to tolerate criticism or to bear frustration. Their personal relationships tend to become confined to other members of the drug addicts' world, and thus they become social outcasts and very lonely people.

In other words, they need—to use the Apostle Paul's words—'to be transformed by the renewing of their minds'. Only God can help them towards this goal. He does—and it is not a distant, despairing target but a nearby practical possibility. Nor is it a negative formula regarding 'needful motivation', or 'Just Say No', or 'a day at a time', or 'care but no cure'. The word of divine power, says God, is near you, even in your heart. The kingdom of God is *not* in words, the Scriptures declare, but in POWER.

One of the first things that God gives to us when we turn

to Him for help, whatever state we are in, is POWER. Paul stated: 'For God has not given us the spirit of fear, but of POWER, and LOVE and a SOUND MIND [or, alternatively, sound judgement, or discipline]'. There is no scope there for negative living. The gift of divine power, divine love and divine judgement is there for the asking. So that we are without excuse in claiming 'I am not able . . .', whatever our circumstances. Paradise is there for the asking.

When the thief dying beside Jesus on the cross said to Him: 'Lord, remember me when you come in your kingdom,' Jesus said to him: 'Truly, I say to you, today you shall be with me in Paradise.' Chemical addiction is an individually chosen way of dealing with reality. Alcoholics Anonymous recognise this element of choice in their dictum: 'I can't. God can. I will let Him do it.'

The first step to spiritual transcendence, therefore, is in recognising and appropriating the preferred divine power of God; the second step is resting in the preferred divine love of God; and the third step is in accepting the preferred divine sound mind of God. The rest is a walk with God through the 'labyrinths of the mind' made in His image; and an exploration with God of the divine purpose for each individual in the world, and the divine purposes of God for the world. That is what Adam and Eve had in an unflawed Paradise.

But it may be that the addict is in too great physiological distress to contemplate even these first simple steps. In Thailand, where they have a million opiate addicts, the Buddhist monks have a system of meditation that is extremely effective in the later stages of rehabilitation; but 90 per cent of the Thai drug addicts never make it to the first few lessons because of their physical distress. Therefore, a satisfactory system of detoxification is the prime requirement in the treatment of all addictions before rehabilitation of any kind can take place.

Nobody should talk about curing addictions who cannot first provide detoxification of the chemically abused conditions. Yet in all the many confused definitions of what constitutes 'cure' of addictions the most misused is that of 'detoxification' itself.

Detoxification means to 'remove the poison', and its etymology is 'to take out an arrow'. What it does NOT mean is its common usage of 'dry-out', or 'cold-turkey', or similar expressions; that is, leaving the poison in while the superficial symptoms are removed. There is no great problem with short-term forms of so-called 'detoxification', as practised in many treatment centres. Like Mark Twain with his giving up cigarette smoking—it can be done many times. The problem to be solved in speaking of a 'cure' is the long-term detoxification; that is, for example, beyond one year from the start of treatment. The standard statistics of all leading forms of treatment, with this for a criterion, indicate ten per cent success.

A leading international authority on the subject of addictions, Dr Avram Goldstein, Professor of Pharmacology at Stanford University, USA, has stated:

> It is still not understood why simple detoxification is so ineffective, but the facts are inescapable . . . As I see it, the reason for the dismal failure of detoxification (the majority of subjects relapse before completing the customary 21 to 30-day treatment) is that the newly detoxified addict, still driven by discomfort, physiologic imbalance, and intense craving, cannot focus attention on the necessary first steps towards rehabilitation, but soon succumbs and starts using again . . .

The prestigious Addiction Research Fund of Ontario, Canada, has tried several varieties of programme, eventually setting up a centre *with no permanent medical staff*. After 50,000 admissions, and no drug treatment whatsoever, no more than 5 per cent had been referred to hospital, and there was not one case of *delirium tremens*. The Coordinator of the ARF programme said: 'Not only do they recover more quickly, but the majority of symptoms don't recur.'

In other words, the solution to the problem of detoxifying addictions lies outside the scope of the present treatment programmes based on outdated medical and psychotherapeutic theories. Many preconceptions and misconceptions regarding the aetiology and treatment of addictions changed in the 1970s, making many current methodologies obsolete, as has been noted earlier in this book.

The new developments probably began in 1972. In a series of 'Skinner Box' experiments investigating causes of drug dependence in rats, a stimulating electrode was permanently implanted in the medial forebrain bundle of the brain so that this bundle of neurons was stimulated whenever the rat pressed a lever, giving a pleasurable sensation. This indicated noradrenaline as the main mediator of reward. Such experiments supported the theory that drugs of dependence induced euphoria by enhancing production of noradrenaline (and related catecholamines) in the brain. The British scientist, Dr H. O. J. Collier, described the significance of the experiments in a 1972 report entitled *The Experimental Analysis of Drug Dependence*:

> An analogy can be drawn between self-injection of a rewarding drug and the behaviour seen when the animal is prepared so that it can stimulate electrically a certain point of its own brain . . . In this situation a rat usually stimulates its brain several times an hour . . . In the most general terms, a multiplication induced by the drug of dependence of some kind of receptor or enzyme, carrier, neurone, or storage site, that handles, or reacts to, an active endogenous substance mediating or moderating neuronal responses, appears to be nearest to explaining dependence . . .

Also in 1972, in Hong Kong, Dr H. L. Wen, a neurosurgeon colleague of Meg's (she was Head of Surgery in the Chinese, 850-bed, Tung Wah Hospital at the time), after visiting mainland China to study the newly developed techniques of electroacupuncture for brain operations, was experimenting with these at the Tung Wah Hospital. In the course of the experiments they noted that they were serendipitously curing patients who, unknown to them, were addicts to various substances. Dr Wen thought the explanation lay in the ancient Chinese practice of acupuncture, but Meg thought it was more likely to be some electrical factor. She began in-depth studies of possible connections between electrical stimulation and drugs. Among other things she had noted that there was a 15-minute delay in the application of the electrical stimulation they were using, and the beginning of the easing of the patients' symptoms, and she deduced that it was due to some unknown chemical factor reacting to the electrical stimulus.

Meg had met, and had corresponded with, Dr Irving Cooper, the 'father of cryogenic surgery' in the curing of Parkinson's disease. He had been experimenting with a variety of electrical impulses for use in intractable epilepsy and spastic paralysis, and he had noted that the cerebellar stimulation was gradually reconditioning the reflex functioning of some brain circuits. Also, he had observed behavioural changes in his patients, even in those who showed little or no physical improvement.

In 1973 Dr Solomon Snyder and researcher Candace Pert of the Johns Hopkins University School of Medicine reported in a scientific journal that they had succeeded in locating in the brain the receptor sites that had attracted opioids. This unleashed a significant increase in the number of related studies in the field of the effects of electrical stimulation.

In 1974 Dr Robert O. Becker of Syracuse University demonstrated how electrodes implanted in the amputation sites of rats could be made to stimulate cell growth and cause some limb growth. At an International Symposium on

Bioelectrochemistry in France he described the system as 'a data transmission system in an analogue fashion using various levels of direct current as its signal. The system interlocks physically with the nervous system and is postulated to be its precursor.'

Then in 1975 Dr Hans Kosterlitz and Dr John Hughes of Aberdeen University, Scotland, identified an endorphin, a natural brain chemical with a molecular structure very similar to the opiates. Almost overnight their discovery triggered an explosion in the understanding of the biochemical basis of behaviour, opening up a whole new vista on the controlling factors behind addiction.

Over succeeding years since then researchers in several countries have uncovered evidence of other brain hormones that mimic psychoactive drugs, from Valium and Angel Dust to the hallucinogens. Almost every mind-altering drug, it is now assumed, has an analogue in the brain. And the precise mixture of neurojuices in this biochemical cocktail can mean the difference between the various 'highs' of tripping, speeding, crashing or smashing. The Paradise Factor.

Meg has described this in one of her books:

> For instance, if you are a jogger, your endorphin production increases dramatically while you are running, and makes you elated. Production of endorphins also increases in response to pain. But when the body becomes accustomed to taking a drug, for example heroin, the endorphins stop being formed because the sites (receptors) on the brain cells where endorphins normally attach to produce their effects are always full of heroin. These sites have to be empty before the brain starts to produce endorphins again ...
>
> To further demonstrate that the endorphin system was involved, the runners were given an injection of naloxone after plasma

measurements were taken at the end of the run.
It was noted, among other findings, that
'naloxone attenuated the elevation in joy and
euphoria ratings that were experienced by the
runners'. This resembles the experiment
described by Professor Avram Goldstein of
Stanford University . . . He gave naloxone to
volunteers who were listening to music which
gave *them* particular pleasure, whether it was
rock or classical. The naloxone took away the
pleasurable experience of the music![1]

Thus there is a distinct correlation between 'motivation
and purposeful behaviour', and the experience of 'elevation in
joy and euphoria' in the application of the joggers to attain
fitness—known as 'jogger's high'. This is also the climactic
'blessedness', or 'happiness', or 'ecstasy', experienced by
spiritual mystics when they commit themselves to prayer and
meditation. Or, in a quieter or less intense form, it is the
experience of satisfaction and joy of the individual who draws
on his or her system of spiritual values to overcome when
confronted by any set of difficult circumstances. The Apostle
Paul described this:

We also *rejoice* in our sufferings, because we
know that suffering produces perseverance;
perseverance, character; and character, hope.
And hope does not disappoint us, because God
has poured out His love into our hearts by the
Holy Spirit, whom He has given us . . .
Therefore, I will boast all the more *gladly* about
my weaknesses, so that Christ's power might
rest upon me. That is why, for Christ's sake, I

1. *Hooked? The New Approach to Drug Cure*, Dr Meg Patterson (London, UK and
Boston, USA: Faber & Faber, 1986; Stuttgart, Germany: Klett-Cotta, 1988): 4th
edition to be published under the new title *The Addicted: The Revolutionary Neuro-
Electric Therapy*, Milton Keynes, UK: Nelson Word, 1994.

delight in weaknesses, in insults, in hardships, in
persecutions, in difficulties. For when I am
weak, then I am strong ... (our italics)

A patient treated by NeuroElectric Therapy (NET), a
year later, wrote an unsolicited letter to Meg describing his
response to the treatment:

Now regarding NET, and an update on my
mental and physical fitness. NET is
miraculous. I've chosen the word carefully and
feel that it most closely reflects my feelings. As
a quick example: as you are aware, Amsterdam
is a 'wide-open' city, where more intoxicating
substances are available than anywhere else.
Had anyone told me that I could remain more
than a week in that city without so much as a
bottle of beer I'd only have scoffed at them,
knowing full well myself that no amount of
will-power could have prevented me for more
than a few days at best from sampling that large
selection of drugs and alcohol that the
metropolitan area offers. I tell you the truth
that I have done that, almost with ease. It still
astonished me to a degree when I recall it ...
I wanted to write to you also about your
theory regarding alcohol as a possible 'curable'
disease. When you first brought up the subject
I was unsure and sceptical, but I have now
altered my outlook on the subject. I believe
you may be correct. Let me explain a bit. I
have always been one who thinks that wine
makes the meal. There simply is no substitute
for good wine with a well-prepared pasta dish,
for example. One night in April Maggie and I
went out to dinner at a quality restaurant and I
had a glass before dinner, and one with dinner,

with no ill side-effects. I went about all this with some trepidation, aware of what the harvest might have been, but my fears were exaggerated . . . I now have an occasional glass with dinner, and sometimes beer with lunch; my fear of falling back into an old pattern is gone. As simply as I can put it is to say the desire just isn't there—indeed, more than that, I feel that more would make me sick. I sometimes wonder if this isn't what 'normal' people feel . . .

Some researchers in the study of alcoholism have discovered a specific substance called *tetrahydroisoquinoline*, or TIQ for short. One of them, Dr Virginia Davis, of Houston, USA, first found TIQ in the brains of alcoholics when she was researching brain cancer. She was surprised to find it in alcoholics, for she had known it was a product of heroin breakdown. It was concluded, therefore, that TIQ caused alcoholics to compulsively drink alcohol.

Then in 1977 Drs Myers and Melchio at Purdue University injected TIQ into the brains of rats which had previously refused alcohol. Following the injection the rats became drunk, stumbled, fell, and experienced tremors and convulsions on withdrawal. Even after several months without alcohol, and without further injections, the rats still preferred alcohol to water.

In 1988 a medical team at the University of California in San Francisco found that white blood cells of alcoholics metabolise alcohol more easily than cells from non-alcoholics, and had lower levels of a fundamental chemical messenger that exists inside cells. The researchers suggested that the findings may indicate why some people find it difficult to control their drinking, and how the tendency to become an alcoholic could be inherited.

Taken together these experiments would appear to indicate that there is both an inherent and inherited chemical factor which predisposed individuals to become addicts. But it should be noted that this is a chemical phenomenon only ('the drug is addictive'), and does not include the other psycho-spiritual factors which contribute to the addictive condition ('the person is addictable') as has been demonstrated above. Chemical abuse is a learned behaviour cultivated by a habitual readiness to resort to mind-altering drugs whenever a painful or stressful situation arises.

There are two basic types of alcoholics, sometimes referred to 'type 1' and 'type 2'. In type 1 alcoholics, one parent is alcoholic, problems usually begin after twenty-five years of age, and there is no record of antisocial behaviour. In type 2, the father only is alcoholic, problems begin in the teens, and are usually associated with antisocial conduct. In a study conducted in the State University of New York Downstate Medical Centre, Dr Henri Begleiter stated: 'You must remember that it is not the *disease* that's inherited, but a propensity or disposition.'

If there is a 'weak, ineffectual, non-disciplining, or absent father' in a family, as addiction statistics show, it follows that the mother must take over the dominant role. This, in turn, produces a series of negative consequences in the children: resentment against the 'weak, etc.' father, and resentment against the dominant and/or indulgent mother who replaces the father, in a descending spiral of interrelated repercussions as the children get older. With an increasing number of single-parent families in permissive Western societies, predominantly matriarchal, it means the percentage of addicts will continue to increase.

In a recent chilling British television documentary, *Spoilt Brats*, it was revealed:

> . . . One young adult of the nineties in three
> will have come from divorced parents, and
> many more will have come from parents whose
> marriage was rocky, or who were maintaining
> the semblance of a marriage until their children
> left home . . . In addition, one teenager in three
> in the nineties will be illegitimate . . .

In this self-indulgent, morally ignorant society created by
the officially sanctioned secular humanist emphases of a
spiritually visionless and valueless education system, the only
escape of the victim is into the illusory world of mind-altering
drugs to change their conceptions of reality.

In a family where one or both parents are chemically
dependent, the percentage of addiction increases
horrendously. Dr David Smith, who founded the famous
Haight-Ashbury Free Medical Clinic in San Francisco during
the height of the drug explosion in 1967, has stated that the
child of an alcoholic parent is 35 times more likely to become
addicted than the child of a non-alcoholic; and that this ratio
soars to 400 if both parents are alcoholic.

What the statistics reveal about chemical addiction is
that the average addict is someone with a 70 per cent chance
of being without a strong and caring father; with a two- to
sevenfold greater likelihood that either parent, or both, are
on some form of mood-altering drugs, such as tranquillisers;
with parents who are either above-average alcohol drinkers,
or who are heavy smokers; with anxiety-provoking home
circumstances of some kind, such as bad relationships, poor
communication, lack of adequate concern; with little self-
confidence, little belief in his or her own identity, little
experience of what passes for 'normal' satisfactions, or
'normal' living; with a history of resorting to legal or illegal
medications in his or her past. In brief, an addict is someone
whose belief or experience or framework of values is

inadequate to their inherited or chosen environment without chemical or behavioural support of some kind.

The Creator has provided in human creatures the physical and psychic means for experiencing the ultimate in pleasure, or paradisal joy—but He ordained the trigger to be a spiritual experience and not a chemical stimulant. When there is no spiritual experience, the chemical stimulant to the human is like that of the rat or the monkey, depressing the lever to get an ever-increasing number of uncontrolled pleasurable stimuli until it kills itself.

Dr Stanton Peele has described the addicts in *Love and Addiction*:

> . . . In these terms then, an addiction exists when a person's attachment to a sensation, an object, or another person is such as to lessen his appreciation of and ability to deal with other things in his environment, or in himself, so that he has become increasingly dependent on that experience as his only source of gratification. A person will be predisposed to addiction to the extent that he cannot establish a meaningful relationship to his environment as a whole, and thus cannot develop a fully elaborated life.

Detoxification by NET, or any other method, is not enough in itself, however, to cure the individual of addiction, even if it accomplishes the desirable goal of clearing the mind and body of the distressing effects of drug abuse, and restores the body to its 'normal' metabolic functioning. If the addiction is more than a compulsion acquired by habit (like so much cigarette smoking) then the addict's need is for appropriate psychospiritual counselling to deal with the underlying problem that led them into chemical dependence in the first place.

The true cure of the addict requires a restructured life, a psychospiritual therapeutic rehabilitation which will provide an adequate framework of values to give not only meaning to the individual and help towards meaningful relationships in family and society, but also an actual, positive, triumphant JOY, even in the most difficult circumstances. In addition, there should be a freedom to choose between options and priorities, a confidence to make the choice knowing that the consequences will be only beneficial in the end, and a sense of responsibility in evaluating all that will flow from the decisions taken. It means providing the addicted individual with an understanding of God and the world in which they live, in order to cure the underlying sense of emptiness, meaninglessness, confusion, depression, anxiety, inadequacy and alienation. The Paradise Factor.

Dr Carl Jung has described in *Man and His Symbols* how instilling a sense of meaning in the individual is more important than any chemical:

> For example, a suitable or comforting word to the patient may have something like a healing effect, which may even affect the glandular secretions. The doctor's words, to be sure, are 'only' vibrations in the air, yet they constitute a particular set of vibrations corresponding to a particular psychic state in the doctor. The words are effective only insofar as they convey a meaning or have a significance. Call it a fiction if you like. Nonetheless it enables us to influence the course of the disease in a far more effective way than with chemical preparations. We can even influence the biochemical processes of the body by it. Whether the fiction arises in me spontaneously, or reaches me from

without by means of some human speech, it can make me ill or cure me . . . Nothing is more effective in the psychic and even psychophysical realms . . .

But it is important to note that, whatever belief system an individual chooses, it must be adequate to meet and to overcome the challenges of the environment in which the individual lives and functions. Otherwise it serves only as a talismanic superstition—a 'rabbit's foot' or decorative crucifix—and not as an effective value system for change in the individual.

CHAPTER 4

Twelve Steps to Paradise

*P*ossibly the most remarkable statement in all of the Scriptures—both Old and New Testaments—are the words. regarding Jesus in the Gospel of John:

> Jesus knew that the Father had put all things under his power, and that he had come from God and was returning to God; so he poured water into a basin and began to wash his disciples' feet . . .

The incident involved took place because Jesus knew that within about two weeks He was going to be put to an abhorrent death because of His teachings, and He was preparing His followers for the consequences following that cataclysmic event. The twelve disciples were with Him in the city of Jerusalem, at the time of the imminent annual celebration of the Jewish Passover Feast. It was a period of political turmoil because of Jewish resentment of the Roman occupation of Jewish territory, and because of the religious antagonism of the professional ecclesiastics against the spiritual teachings of Jesus—especially the conception of Jesus as the promised 'Messiah', or 'Christ', the 'Anointed of God'—and His denunciation of ecclesiastical ritualistic tyranny and personal religious hypocrisy.

With national controversy raging over the consequences of this long-prophesied appearance of God's Messianic

messenger on earth—Would God overthrow the Roman
Empire of the Caesars? Would God restore the Jewish Empire
of King David?—the twelve obscure men from rural Galilee
in the small and despised nation of Israel were gathered in an
upper room of a house in Jerusalem listening to what,
according to their chosen Galilean Rabbi, were His last words
before death. The simple evening meal had been served and,
as they sat around the table talking about their recent
evangelistic activities, Jesus rose from the table. The
conversation died as they noted the deliberately chosen
actions of their acknowledged leader:

> Jesus knew that the Father had *put all things under
> his power*, and that *he had come from God* and was
> *returning to God*; so he poured water into a basin
> and *began to wash his disciples' feet* . . .

Why would the Messiah, 'the Anointed of God', at the
moment of His own greatest divine assurance, and at the time
of His followers' lowest prophetic conviction, choose this
action to convince them of His essential divinity and their
potential association with Him? They were bewildered as
much by what He was asking them to do in submitting to His
service, as they were by His doing it. Peter, ever the first to
react, argued against having his feet washed by Jesus; and
Jesus confused him and the others even more by asserting:
'You do not realise now what I am doing, but later you will
understand.'

To emphasise the importance of His action He said to
Peter: 'Unless I wash you, you have no part with me.' It was
obvious that it was not just the ceremony of feet-washing that
Jesus had in mind with that remark—that would have been
done earlier on entering the house, or room—and with that
He added: 'A person who has had a bath needs only to wash
his feet; his whole body is clean. And you are clean, though
not every one of you.' The writer of the Scriptures adds here:
'For he knew who was going to betray him, and that was why

he said not every one was clean.' The 'cleansing', therefore, Jesus had in mind was for a sinful act, and motivation for the act.

It was clear to all in the room that there were undercurrents and tensions, some caused by bewilderment and some by ignorance and some by personality clashes and ambitions. But what was uppermost in most minds was Jesus' prophecies that at some point they would all forsake Him, and one would even betray Him. The necessity for being spiritually 'clean' had also been strongly asserted by Jesus, when He bluntly told Peter: 'Unless I wash you, you have no part with me.' Note that it was the unthinking, impetuous Peter whom Jesus openly rebuked, and not the silent renegade Judas.

Within a few minutes all would know that Judas was the betrayer, but only Jesus knew that Peter would also betray Him in the approaching crisis—and the others would all return to their homes and jobs. The thought of submitting self-will to the needs of others, even at the risk of personal humiliation and death, was too difficult for even the closest followers of Jesus to accept.

When He had finished washing their feet, and had returned to His place at the table, He continued:

> Do you understand what I have done for you? You call me 'Teacher' and 'Lord', and rightly so, for that is what I am. Now that I, your Lord and Teacher, have washed your feet, you should also wash one another's feet. I have set you an example that you should do as I have done for you. I tell you the truth, no servant is greater than his master, nor is a messenger greater than the one who sent him.

Jesus at this point was aware, as we have noted above, that 'the Father had put all things under his power', that He had come from 'equality with God' and was soon returning to 'being glorified with the glory he had with the Father from the beginning'. Yet He wanted His twelve obscure followers to recognise, in this time of crisis, that 'power over all things' was contingent upon being willingly and understandingly submissive to a higher will, and not upon the personally exercised 'lordship' over others. If they could not accept this, then they 'had no part with him', and had no message for the world. Judas did not accept it, and he left the room to launch the final events of Jesus' life and death on earth.

At the start of the evening meal, the Scriptures said, 'the devil had already *prompted* Judas Iscariot, son of Simon, to betray Jesus'. By the end of the meal, they record, 'as soon as Judas took the bread, Satan *entered* into him'. Within the space of an hour or so Judas had passed from being tempted to a course of action, differing from that being propounded by Jesus, to one of being unalterably and diabolically opposed. For thirty pieces of silver Judas tried to change the course of divine history, because he disagreed with submission to a Higher Authority and chose the way of Satan —who 'chose to reign in hell rather than serve in heaven'.

When it came to the time of Peter's betrayal, in the courtyard of the High Priest's house following on Jesus' arrest, his reaction was totally different to that of Judas. When he realised what he had done, he 'went out and wept bitterly'. He remembered the words and actions of Jesus, and knew that failure was not the end of all things, but an opportunity to begin again. A humble and a contrite heart God would not despise. Even though he could not undo the act of denial and betrayal, he could redeem his past by changing himself. He could never erase the fact of failure at a time of crisis, but he could atone for the failure by becoming a changed man. As Frankl describes the process psychotherapeutically in *Man's Search for Meaning*: 'By repentance, a man who failed by a deed and cannot remove its outcome, detaches himself from his deed and thereby, from himself. He cannot change what has happened, but he can change himself. He may grow morally.'

How Peter 'grew morally' afterwards is a matter of recorded

history. He went out to the world, at Jesus' command, to 'feed the lambs' and 'feed the sheep', and gave his life in doing it. Before his death he wrote with sublime assurance:

> [God's] divine power has given us everything we need for life and godliness through our knowledge of him who called us by his own glory and goodness. Through these he has given us his very great and precious promises, so that through them you may participate in the divine nature and escape the corruption in the world caused by evil desires.
>
> For this very reason, make every effort to add to your faith, goodness; and to goodness, knowledge; and to knowledge, self-control; and to self-control, perseverance; and to perseverance, godliness; and to godliness, brotherly kindness; and to brotherly kindness, love. For if you possess these qualities in increasing measure, they will keep you from being ineffective and unproductive . . . If you do these things, you will never fall, and *you will receive a rich welcome into the eternal kingdom of our Lord and Saviour Jesus Christ.* (our italics)

Paradise regained.

In other words, what Peter was saying was that if these eight qualities were pursued and possessed 'in increasing measure', the universally prevalent threats of 'emptiness and meaninglessness' would be overcome—*and an entrance into Paradise would be effected.* And God had provided 'everything we need for life and godliness' through Jesus Christ. Finally, by keeping these basic qualities 'you will never fall'. All this from a man who—some thirty years before—not only didn't believe Jesus could rise from the dead, but who denied with oaths and curses any association with Him at the time of His greatest personal crisis!

The Apostle Paul had a similar experience. An arrogant intellectual Pharisee, whose religious bigotry drove him to put all dissenting men and women to prison or death, his encounter with Jesus on the Damascus road not only changed his own nature but spiritually revolutionised the world in his own time and forever afterwards. From his personal experience he could attest that one who was characterised as 'chief of sinners' could be changed into 'Christ-likeness' and experience the Paradise Factor. He knew what he was talking about when he said:

> Put to death, therefore, whatever belongs to your earthly nature: sexual immorality, impurity, lust, evil desires and greed, which is idolatry . . . You used to walk in these ways, in the life you once lived. But now you must rid yourself of all such things as these: anger, rage, malice, slander and filthy language from your lips. Do not lie to each other, *since you have taken off your old self* with its practices, and *have put on the new self*, which is being renewed in knowledge in the image of its Creator. (our italics)

From the beginning of time, when He placed the first parents of humankind in an earthly Paradise, it was God's expressed purpose that men and women should be perfect creatures—'made in His image'—reflecting the divine nature. From the time of their fall from high place and calling through disobedience it has been God's primary purpose—'the mystery of His will'—to restore fallen men and women to the state of paradisal perfection that will permit them to enter and enjoy God's paradisal presence without judgement and without fear. This is how Paul described the paradisal experience:

> Praise be to the God and Father of our Lord

> Jesus Christ, who has *blessed us in the heavenly
> realms with every spiritual blessing in Christ*. For
> he chose us in him before the creation of the
> world *to be holy and blameless in his sight*. (our
> italics)

The command of God through a succession of His
servants in the Old Testament is: 'You shall be holy as the
Lord your God is holy.' And the command of Jesus to His
disciples in the New Testament is: 'You shall be perfect as
your Father in heaven is perfect.' And the Apostle Paul,
founder of the early Church, declared as his aim: '. . . to
present every man perfect in Christ Jesus . . . that you may
stand perfect and complete in all the will of God'. Paul was
not writing to devout believers, but to the church in Corinth
that had 'many who have sinned earlier and have not
repented of the impurity, sexual sin and debauchery in which
they have indulged'.

Paul's goal for himself, as well as for others, was 'to be
perfect'. He could say, however:

> Not that I have already been made perfect, but
> I press on . . . toward the goal to win the prize
> for which God has called me heavenward . . .
> the Lord Jesus Christ, who, by the power that
> enables him to bring everything under his
> control, *will transform our lowly bodies so that
> they will be like his glorious body*. (our italics)

The Paradise Factor.

It is the gap between this divinely implanted consciousness of attainable perfection, and individual awareness of
falling short of it, that produces the *deceptio visus*, or distorted,
Paradise Factor of the addict. We *know* we are capable of
walking with God. We *know* that—like Paul—we have the
mystical capacity to be caught up to 'the third heaven' to see
and hear things we cannot describe. We may even *know*

occasions when we have been 'kissed by God', and the intoxication was beyond all wine and other stimulants— 'Your love is better than wine.' But, more than all of these, we *know* we have not attained to the paradisal perfection provided by God, which hovers at the edge of our consciousness.

Paul, the founder of the Christian Church, never made it, so why should we expect to succeed where he failed? Nevertheless, he set for himself, and for all others, a divine goal that held promise on earth of the great things that lay ahead. Of his own paradisal experience he said:

> . . . caught up to paradise, and heard inexpressible things, things that man is not permitted to tell. I will boast about a man like that, but I will not boast about myself, except about my weaknesses . . . To keep me from becoming conceited because of these surpassingly great revelations, there was given me a thorn in the flesh, a messenger of Satan to torment me. Three times I pleaded with the Lord to take it away from me. But he said to me, 'My grace is sufficient for you, for my power is made perfect in weakness.' Therefore I will boast all the more gladly about my weaknesses, so that Christ's power may rest on me. That is why, for Christ's sake, I delight in weaknesses, in insults, in hardships, in persecutions, in difficulties. For when I am weak, then I am strong.

For Paul, the Paradise Factor was not something to be sought or attained in order to be delivered from the stresses of everyday living and witnessing to the presence and glory of God. The 'inexpressible things' and 'surpassingly great revelations' were not an end in themselves—as, for example, the chemically-induced experiences were to Huxley, Leary, and the assorted gurus of the 1960s and '70s. They were an unsought gift from God to indicate the 'riches of the glory of his inheritance . . . which he wrought in Christ when he raised him from the dead and set him at his own right hand in the heavenly places'. They were part of the 'joy unspeakable and full of glory' which, Paul affirmed, 'eye has not seen, nor ear heard, neither have entered into the heart of man what God has prepared for them that love him. But God has revealed them to us by his Spirit; for the Spirit searches all things, yes, the deep things of God.' Most of all, Paul understood from his personal experience that the paradisal gift from God was inextricably associated with personal weakness, struggle, confrontation and transformation.

What is important to note is that *the paradisal blessings were attainable by all.* They were not the esoteric prerogatives of a few isolated mystics. It is important always to keep in mind when Paul speaks of these experiences that he is writing to a group of diverse, unhappy, rebellious, stubborn, discriminatory, drunken, self-opinionated, sexually promiscuous, professing Christians in Corinth, the most licentious 'sin-city' of the times. But, also, they were 'the church of God in Corinth, those sanctified in Christ Jesus and *called to be holy,* together with *all those everywhere* who call on the name of our Lord Jesus Christ—their Lord and ours'.

Paul saw them as they were, as they could be, and as they were meant to be by God. It did not matter to Paul that the world they lived in was dominated by an unparalleled totalitarian military dictatorship; that the world leaders in politics and philosophy and religion were publicly recognised as unspeakably corrupt; that the people of that time were sated with state-supplied pleasures to keep them occupied. The emperors of Rome hardly needed a secret police because, to keep the people occupied and distracted from protest, they supplied them with free meals, frequent gifts of money, and as many as 150 days of spectator sports a year. The State's Satanic counterfeit of the Paradise Factor.

Neither the Apostle Paul nor John nor any of the others devised a new religion, or religious institution, following on the death of Christ. They were all Jews; practising Jews as Jesus' brother, James, showed in his devout manner of life that was respected by all Jews of that time. What was new, as Paul demonstrated so effectively, was that 'the substance' (in the coming of Jesus into the world as God's Messiah) had replaced 'the shadow' (of the Old Testament symbols and prophecies concerning His coming). The physical Tabernacle, or Tent of Meeting, and the Temple, as places where God could be met under certain stringent conditions of sacrifices and laws, were replaced with the coming of Christ—who fulfilled all God's legal requirements—as God's sacrificial Lamb, and God's public declaration that 'This is my beloved Son in whom I am well pleased.' With Jesus as an acceptable High Priest offering His body and work as a vicarious sacrifice on behalf of others, there was no further need for animal sacrifices and buildings to approach God. The way to Paradise was now open—but it had a narrow gate! Writing to the non-Jews of Ephesus, Paul said:

> But now in Christ Jesus you who once were far away have been brought near by the blood of Christ. For he himself is our peace, who has made the two one and has destroyed the barrier, the dividing wall of hostility, by abolishing in his flesh the law with its commandments and regulations. His purpose was to create in himself one new man out of the two, thus making peace, and in this one body to reconcile both of them to God through the cross, by which he put to death their hostility. He came and preached peace to you who were far away and peace to those who were near. For through him we both have access to the Father by one Spirit.
> Consequently, you are no longer foreigners

and aliens, but fellow-citizens with God's
people and members of God's household, built
on the foundation of the apostles and prophets,
with Christ Jesus himself as the chief
cornerstone. In him the whole building is
joined together and rises to become a holy
temple in the Lord. And in him you too are
being built together to become a dwelling in
which God lives by his Spirit.

That is what Jesus Christ did by the offering up of
Himself on behalf of others to God—He eliminated ALL
barriers, between all nations and Jews, and between Jews and
non-Jews and God. For the Jews also had alienated
themselves from God by their disobedience and
rebelliousness. Now there was no longer a dividing wall of
hostility, and in Himself Jesus has created 'one new man out
of two, thus making peace'. All it needs is for an individual to
accept the free gift of God. The Paradise Factor.

The Twelve Steps to Paradise

The 'Twelve Steps to Paradise'—to which the atoning
work of Christ on the cross is the 'gateway'—have been
magnificently delineated in the New Testament book of
Hebrews. Written by an anonymous Jewish Christian, it lays
out in detailed comprehensive grandeur the means by which
God takes the most degraded individual and makes him or
her into a perfect creature fit to share the paradisal presence
of God.

Step One: *The Epitome of Perfection*
The writer establishes Jesus as God's historical epitome of
perfection to accomplish His eternal purpose in the world,
and on the basis of which any individual is able to enter the
presence of God and share in the divine inheritance:

> In the past God spoke to our forefathers
> through the prophets at many times and in
> various ways, but in these last days he has
> spoken to us by his Son, whom he appointed
> heir of all things, and through whom he made
> the universe. The Son is the radiance of God's
> glory and the exact representation of his being,
> sustaining all things by his powerful word. After
> he had provided purification for sins, he sat
> down at the right hand of the Majesty in
> heaven. So he became as much superior to the
> angels as the name he has inherited is superior
> to theirs (Hebrews chapter 1).

Step Two: Made Perfect Through Suffering

The writer demonstrates how even Jesus, although the
beloved Son of God, had to be made perfect through the
process of suffering:

> We see Jesus . . . now crowned with glory and
> honour because he suffered death, so that by
> the grace of God he might taste death for
> everyone. In bringing many sons to glory, it
> was fitting that God, for whom and through
> whom everything exists, should make the
> author of their salvation perfect through
> suffering. Both the one who makes men holy
> and those who are made holy are of the same
> family (Hebrews chapter 2).

Step Three: Obedience, the Key to Perfection

For those accepted by God through the gift of love and grace,
and members of the same family of Christ, being made perfect
through suffering, being 'made holy' means 'living differently
as God lives differently':

> Therefore, holy brothers, who share in the

heavenly calling, fix your thoughts on Jesus, the
apostle and high priest whom we confess
. . . We are his house, if we hold on to our
courage and the hope of which we boast . . .
See to it, brothers, that none of you has a
sinful, unbelieving heart that turns away from
the living God. But encourage one another
daily . . . so that none of you may be hardened
by sin's deceitfulness. We have come to share
in Christ if we hold firmly till the end the
confidence we had at first . . . (Hebrews chapter
3).

Step Four: Perfect Priest to Help Imperfect People

Disobedience is the greatest cause of lapses in perfection in
individuals professing to follow Christ. The writer shows how
God was angry with those who rebelled against His provision
for them, and 'they were not able to enter (enjoy the
paradisal Promised Land), because of their unbelief'. To
avoid this state of affairs, the writer continues, it is necessary
for the individual to both know and obey the commands of
God. In order to accomplish this high goal God has provided
both the Scriptures and a sympathetic high priest to help us:

For the word of God is living and active.
Sharper than any double-edged sword, it
penetrates even to dividing soul and spirit,
joints and marrow; it judges the thoughts and
attitudes of the heart. Nothing in all creation
is hid from God's sight. Everything is
uncovered and laid bare before the eyes of him
to whom we must give account.

Therefore, since we have a great high priest
who has gone through the heavens, Jesus the
Son of God, let us hold firmly to the faith we
profess. For we do not have a high priest who is
unable to sympathise with our weaknesses, but

> we have one who has been tempted in every
> way, just as we are—yet was without sin. Let us
> then approach the throne of grace with
> confidence, so that we may receive mercy and
> find grace to help us in our time of need
> (Hebrews chapter 4).

Step Five: Perfection Reached Through Prayer and Training

The function of a high priest is to sympathise tenderly, deal gently 'with those who are ignorant and going astray', and to 'offer sacrifices'. Jesus fulfilled these criteria, the writer says, because:

> . . . During the days of Jesus' life on earth he
> offered up prayers and petitions with loud cries
> and tears to the one who could save him from
> death, and he was heard because of his reverent
> submission. Although he was a son, he learned
> obedience from what he suffered and, once
> made perfect, he became the source of eternal
> salvation for all who obey him and was
> designated by God to be a high priest . . .

The writer goes on to agree that this is hard teaching, but that the readers are to blame for any lack of understanding because they choose to be 'infants living on milk' and not 'mature on solid food'. The latter, he insists, have acquired their abilities 'by constant use of training [of their senses, or minds] to distinguish good from evil'. So, prayers are heard because of 'reverent submission'; and spiritual maturity is obtained through training the mind in perception (Hebrews chapter 5).

Step Six: Perfection for All is Divine Goal

The elementary teachings about Christ, said the writer, are for the intellectual and spiritual infants with no interest beyond the theological milk they suck. It is the intellectually and spiritually mature who reach for and 'go on to perfection':

> God is not unjust; he will not forget your work and the love you have shown him as you have helped his people and continue to help them. We want each of you to show this same diligence to the very end, in order to make your hope sure. We do not want you to become lazy, but to imitate those who through faith and patience inherit what has been promised.

The writer drew attention to the fact that it was God's custom to establish His stated commitments by an oath to make them doubly sure:

> . . . Because God wanted to make the unchanging nature of his purpose very clear to the heirs of what was promised, he confirmed it with an oath. God did this so that, by two unchangeable things [His word and His oath] in which it was impossible for God to lie, we who have fled to take hold of the hope offered to us may be greatly encouraged. We have this hope as an anchor for the soul, firm and secure . . . (Hebrews chapter 6).

Step Seven: Imperfect Law, Perfect High Priest
The Jewish writer, addressing his fellow Jews, argued from the Mosaic Scriptures that, if perfection for individuals could have been attained through the divinely ordained Levitical priesthood, why was there still need for another priest to come—for example, Melchizedek, who was not of the order of Aaron? The former regulations were set aside, he maintained, because they were weak and useless—the Mosaic Law making nothing and no one perfect—and a better hope was introduced by God to permit men and women to draw

near to Him, one who had been made perfect through suffering, obedience and faith. This was accomplished by Jesus, God's own High Priest, meeting all the divine requirements on our behalf—which the Law could not by its very nature:

> Such a high priest meets our need—one who is holy, blameless, pure, set apart from sinners, exalted above the heavens . . . For the Law appoints as high priests men who are weak; but the oath [God's new covenant], which came after the Law, appointed the Son, who has been made perfect forever.

This act of God in grace meant also that there was no further need to have 'sacred' buildings or animals or rituals or priesthood, for the way into God's presence had been opened by the work of God's Son and direct approach into the divine presence was now possible and encouraged. With Jesus as High Priest, no earthly mediating priest was necessary to act on behalf of other men and women (Hebrews chapter 7).

Step Eight: God's Perfect Covenant
This ministry that Jesus had received from God the Father is superior in every way

> . . . as the covenant of which he is mediator is superior to the old one, and it is founded on better promises. For if there had been nothing wrong with the first covenant, no place would have been sought for another . . . 'I will put my laws in their minds and write them on their hearts. I will be their God and they will be my people . . . they will all know me, from the least of them to the greatest. For I will forgive their wickedness and will remember their sins no more.' By calling this covenant 'new', he has

made the first obsolete; and what is obsolete
and ageing will soon disappear.

The laws of God are no longer external to the individual
but, through the receiving of God's free gift of forgiveness of
sins in Jesus Christ, these are now communicated directly to
the minds and hearts of believers by the Spirit of God so that
they become children of God and able to know God and
reflect His divine purposes (Hebrews chapter 8).

Step Nine: *Perfection Eternally*

The new life under the new covenant gifted by God is not for
this lifetime only, but for ever. The writer points out to his
fellow-Jews how, under the old covenant, neither the priests
nor the sacrifices were perfect. But Christ, in offering up
Himself on our behalf to the eternal God, as the eternal Son
through the eternal Spirit, 'cleansed your conscience from
dead works to serve the living God . . . that those who have
been called might receive the promise of eternal inheritance'.
This eternal inheritance of life in the Spirit is secured by the
presence of Christ in heaven at God's right hand acting as
advocate on behalf of all those who are linked to Him by
faith in the present, and who look for His return to earth a
second time to share His spiritual kingdom (Hebrews chapter
9).

Step Ten: *Made Perfect by Holy Action*

Since the Law by its very nature was imperfect, the writer
argued, it could not make any of its practitioners perfect, as
God required. It could only perform an inadequate educative
function at best. It was like a school-teacher pointing forward
to Christ. Similarly, animals who were led unwillingly to the
slaughter were also inadequate sacrifices to placate a God
demanding perfection from alienated creatures made in His
image. What was needed was a sinless, willing human
creature acceptable to God, to act on behalf of the whole
sinning human race.

Christ volunteered to be that offering, to be the 'propitiation'—the 'debt-payer'—on behalf of all those 'debtors to God'. It was this willingness to become the 'scapegoat', to submit Himself in a daily sacrifice of His own will in order to do only the will of God, that becomes, at the same time, both the atonement for our sins and the example for us to follow:

> Then he said, 'Here I am, I have come to do your will' . . . And by that will we have been made holy through the sacrifice of the body of Jesus Christ once for all . . . because by one sacrifice he has made perfect forever those who are being made holy.

To be made holy, therefore, means to be subject to God in a daily sacrificial obedience to His will as demonstrated by Jesus. This is 'the gospel of Christ . . . the power of God to every one who believes' (Hebrews chapter 10).

Step Eleven: Faith, the Perfecting Process

It is the power of God, which brought Jesus Christ from death to His right hand, which is made available to every believer in order to transform them into the perfected creatures purposed by God 'according to His good pleasure'. This faith, the writer says, 'is being sure of what we hope for, and certain of what we do not see . . . By faith we understand that the universe was formed at God's command, so that what is seen was not made out of what is visible.' He then goes on to list all who were Old Testament examples of those 'whose weakness was turned to strength' by their exercise of faith in God:

> These were all commended for their faith, yet none of them received what was promised. *God had planned something better for us so that only together with us would they be made perfect* (Hebrews chapter 11, our italics).

Step Twelve: *Perfection of Divine Discipline*

What God planned was for all to be perfect together in Paradise. With Jesus as the goal—'Let us fix our eyes on Jesus, the author and perfecter of our faith, who for the JOY set before him endured the cross, scorning its shame, and sat down at the right hand of God'—the writer encourages all to submit to the discipline of love in the perfecting process through life:

> God disciplines us for our good, that we may share his holiness. No discipline seems pleasant at the time, but painful. Later on, however, it produces a harvest of righteousness and peace for those who have been trained by it.

This sharing of the holiness of God, the writer asserts, means Paradise for all:

> But you have come to Mount Zion, to the heavenly Jerusalem, the city of the living God. You have come to thousands and thousands of angels in joyful assembly, to the church of the firstborn, whose names are written in heaven. You have come to God, the judge of all men, to the spirits of righteous men made perfect, to Jesus the mediator of a new covenant . . . (Hebrews chapter 12).

The ultimate Paradise Factor. The antithesis to the fearsome Law and Commandments delivered to Moses on Mount Sinai, the place of fear:

> For you have not come to the mountain that may be touched and that burned with fire, and to blackness and darkness and tempest, and the sound of a trumpet and the voice of words,

so that those who heard it begged that the word should not be spoken to them any more . . . and so terrifying was the sight that Moses said, 'I am exceedingly afraid and trembling' . . .

Since we are receiving a kingdom which cannot be shaken, let us have grace, by which we may serve God acceptably with reverence and *godly fear*. For our God is a consuming fire. (our italics)

It was *fear* that kept the Jews from enjoying the Paradise of God under the Old Covenant—but it was the wrong kind of fear. It was fear based on unbelief in the promises of God. It was fear that arose from a guilty conscience, conscious that the individual really preferred present self-gratification to future paradisal pleasures. And it is the wrong kind of fear that still keeps people in the twentieth century from experiencing the true paradisal joys.

It was from this Satan-induced fear, and its ultimate aspect in the fear of death controlled by Satan, that God sent Jesus to remove in the offering up of Himself on the cross: '. . . that through death he might destroy him who had the power of death, that is, the devil, and release those who through fear of death were all their lifetime subject to bondage . . .'

So it became possible for everyone to pass through death to transfiguration, and the path to that goal is bedevilled by fear and only successfully negotiated by 'godly fear'—the essential prerogative to acquiring Paradise.

John Bunyan, while in prison writing his *Pilgrim's Progress*, viewed man's life as a journey, with Christians travelling from the City of Destruction to the glory and resplendent majesty of Heaven, the entrance of which is barred by a river:

This River has been a Terror to many, yea the thoughts of it also have often frighted me. But now methinks I stand easie, my Foot is fixed upon that, upon which the Feet of the Priests that bare the Ark of the Covenant stood while Israel went over this Jordan. The Waters indeed are to the Palate bitter, and to the Stomack cold; yet the thoughts of what I am going to, and of the Convoy that waits for me on the other side, doth lie as a glowing Coal at my Heart.

I see my self now at the end of my Journey, my toilsom Days are ended. I am going to see that Head that was Crowned with Thorns, and that Face that was spit upon for me . . .

But glorious it was, to see how the upper Region was filled with Horses and Chariots, with Trumpeters and Pipers, with Singers, and Players on stringed Instruments, to welcome the Pilgrims as they went up and followed one another in at the beautiful Gate of the City.

Paradise.

CHAPTER 5

The Fear of Death

Science in the twentieth century is based on the premise 'we must live' at almost any cost, and devotes itself to searching for the means to do this acceptably. The Bible, on the other hand, is based on the premise that 'we all must die', and devotes itself to providing the means to understand and face this.

Despite the inordinate attention paid by scientists to this subject, Sir Peter Medawar, the late noted British scientist and a specialist in ageing, said:

> Little advance has been made recently in prolonging the life-span, but that is not surprising. In former days a person who reached the age of sixty had to have been pretty tough—natural selection had been operating throughout life and the weaker would have fallen. There is no God-given parameter called the normal lifespan; the lifespan is what we cause it to be. Lifespan can be prolonged in mice and rats, but only by using means which it is not easy to see as applicable to man. If a method were devised to prolong the span then our conception of the right and proper age to die would change accordingly.

Be that as it may—and Sir Peter Medawar did not live long enough to prove his thesis—the average age of men and women is still, as the Bible says, 'three-score years and ten'.

At the beginning of the twentieth century, in 1901 to be exact, a man who survived to the age of 70 could expect to live to 78, and a woman who lived to 70 could expect to live to 79. At the end of the century the man can only expect to live one year more, and the woman three years more. So the Bible is still more accurate than the scientists. What is increasing is the number of people, both men and women, who reach 70 or over.

Strangely enough, despite the common apprehension of the experience of death, it appears that when it becomes time to face it most people do so with apathy. The renowned physician Sir William Osler, who died in 1919, said that he had kept careful records of the death-beds of 500 people, and concluded: 'Ninety suffered bodily pain or distress of one sort or another, eleven showed mental apprehension, two positive terror, and one expressed spiritual exaltation, one bitter remorse . . . The great majority gave no sign, one way or another; their death was a sleep and a forgetting.'

In a civilised, affluent and basically godless Western setting, under the supervision of a noted physician, this reaction might be taken as the norm. But put a number of people into a situation facing certain death and the response could be considerably different—as, for example, in what is known as 'the Black Hole of Calcutta', when 145 men and one woman were imprisoned together in one small room about eighteen feet square. A record of a survivor, Mr Holwell, reads:

> . . . [In the heat and cramped conditions] many were in the act of dying. Mr Holwell suggested they should take off their clothes to afford more room. An effort was made to fan the air with their hats, but the exertion could not be borne . . . The situation was now frightful. The weak were trodden to death . . . Some became furiously delirious; others vainly sought to provoke the sentinels to fire upon them. Thirst

became excessive . . . but in time the natural love of life prevailed over all other feelings. The crowd eagerly pressed to the window and, seizing the iron bars, climbed on his shoulders. He begged for his life . . . his thirst was excessive, and he endeavoured to allay it by sucking the moisture from his shirt . . . The despair became unbounded and terrible, and they all called for air . . . then suddenly the noise ceased, and the greater part laid down and died . . .

To some, the report of Sir William Osler might be a comfort, and even an exoneration of a life lived in the conviction that there was nothing after death. As Solomon the Wise wrote in Ecclesiastes:

For what happens to the sons of men also happens to animals; one thing befalls them: as one dies, so dies the other. Surely, they all have one breath; man has no advantage over animals, for all is vanity. All go to one place: all are from the dust, and all return to dust.

If Solomon had ended his despairing cry there it would have pleased the nihilists of history; but he continued: 'Who knows the spirit of the sons of men, which goes upward, and the spirit of the animal, which goes down to the earth?'

It was the Apostle Paul who provided the explicit answer, when he wrote in 1 Corinthians 2:7–16:

We speak the wisdom of God in a mystery, the hidden wisdom which God ordained before the ages for our glory . . . 'Eye has not seen, nor ear heard, nor have entered into the heart of man the things which God has prepared for those who love Him' . . . But God has revealed them

> to us through His Spirit . . . For what man
> knows the things of a man except the spirit of
> the man which is in him? Even so no one
> knows the things of God except the Spirit of
> God . . . We have the mind of Christ . . .

Jesus Christ removed the veil between life and death when He passed through the experience and rose to be seated at God's right hand; from there to send the Spirit of God to guide us into all truth, and reveal all things of the Father God to us. It was for this reason that Paul could declare: 'O Death, where is your sting? O Hell, where is your victory? The sting of death is sin . . . But thanks be to God, who gives us the victory through our Lord Jesus Christ . . .'

To the believer in Jesus Christ death is not—or should not be—'a sleep and a forgetting', something which happens to beasts; but a triumphant passing through the curtain into the indescribable glories of Paradise.

It is the conflict between the known fate of 'the mortal', and the unknown destiny of 'the immortal', which creates the tension and fears of the individual facing death. The act of dissolution of the body when the moment of death arrives is usually faced, as we have seen, with either equanimity or apathy, depending on the individual's state of mind. There is the natural fear of the immediate consequences, such as being buried alive, or being burned alive, if one is not really dead but only in some form of coma.

But the greater fear—whether expressed to death-bed inquirers or not—is of the unknown experience lying beyond the fact of death. However much we push it away, every person at some time is conscious that death lies just over the horizon—a distant and squirming recognition when one is young, a near and anxious expectation when one is older.

Dylan Thomas, the Welsh poet and alcohol addict, was both obsessed and repelled by the thought of death:

I have longed to move away
From the hissing of the spent lie
And the old terrors' continual cry
Growing more terrible as the day
Goes over the hill into the deep sea;
I have longed to move away
From the repetition of salutes,
For there are ghosts in the air
And ghostly echoes on paper
And the thunder of calls and notes.

On the death of his father he raged impotently:

Do not go gentle into that good night,
Old age should burn and rave at close of day;
Rage, rage against the dying of the light . . .

And, you, my father, there on the sad height,
Curse, bless, me now with your fierce tears, I
      pray.
Do not go gentle into that good night.
Rage, rage against the dying of the light.

There seems little doubt that it is the individual's beliefs which determine his or her attitude at the time of death. When George was in Tibet he discovered that, to the Tibetans, the fact of death was linked with their belief in an after-death state of forty-nine days known as *bardo*. The Tibetans maintained that it was the unwillingness to face death with understanding, and the undue emphasis which people placed on the physical body and its associations, which produced fear and morbidity. They prepared for death, as we shall see in a later chapter, with carefully controlled rituals, forms, prayers, services and ceremonies as laid out in their classic *Bardo Thodol*, or *The Tibetan Book of the Dead*.

The Islam attitude to death is really a mixture of Jewish, Christian and Zoroastrian ideas regarding life after death. In Islam there are seven heavens and seven hells. Some Muslims believe that no Muslim ever goes to hell, while others believe that some Muslims do, and remain there in the seventh hell until they are redeemed by a prophet, when they pass to Paradise.

In the West the general attitude to death in the past was strongly influenced by Judaeo-Christian beliefs. Following on the so-called Enlightenment ushered in by the French Revolution and atheists like Descartes and Voltaire (although even Voltaire said, 'We begin to die as soon as we are born.') there was a dramatic decline in the general public belief in the Christian Scriptures. There were, of course, the great evangelistic campaigns conducted by charismatic Christian leaders such as Wesley, Finney and Edwards.

These preachers were very conscious of the fact of death and it coloured the presentation of the gospel they preached—the imminence and agonies of hell, and the certainties and glories of heaven. Jonathan Edwards declared:

> For death, with the pains and agonies with
> which it is usually brought on, is not merely a
> limiting of existence, but is a most terrible
> calamity; and to such a creature as man,
> capable of conceiving of immortality, and made
> with so earnest a desire after it, and capable of
> foresight and of reflection on approaching
> death, and that has such an extreme dread of it,
> is a calamity above all others terrible, to such as
> are able to reflect upon it . . .

The twentieth century has produced no comparable great preachers on the subjects of heaven and hell mainly because of the lack of public knowledge of the Christian Scriptures, and the unwillingness of Christian preachers to preach on an unknown and unpopular subject. The Bible is still the world's best-selling book, but it would appear that very few people bother to read it, let alone observe its teachings.

The most sought-after public speaker on death in the West is Dr Elizabeth Kubler-Ross, a Swiss-born psychiatrist, who has made a special study of death and dying. She is very popular in holistic circles in the United States of America. On the occasions when we have heard her lecture she has avoided being specific in Christian terms regarding death and the afterlife, being evasive even under questioning, and emphasising a pantheistic conception of 'light', 'bliss' and 'spirit beings'. Dr Kubler-Ross posits a fivefold reaction to imminent death: defiance, anger, bargaining, depression and acceptance (which we shall look at in a subsequent chapter).

In the United States, it is claimed, ninety per cent of those dying wish to be told of it; and ninety per cent of the doctors advise against it. In these circumstances death becomes something of a lottery: am I dying or am I not? Very few have the strong conviction of Socrates that 'the inner voice' he had known during his lifetime had ceased, so he knew his death was now imminent and he could face it. But to some—even when they are not told by doctors, or family, or friends—there arises a knowledge that their time to leave this life has come. Unfortunately, even this consciousness is often blurred and deadened by the well-meaning intervention of doctors in prescribing drugs to 'give peace of mind' to the individual.

How much more considerate and helpful is the treatment prescribed by Dr Cecily Saunders, of London's St John's Hospice (which cares almost exclusively for the incurable), that involves regarding the dying inmates as at their most emotionally and psychologically mature. She adds: 'You remember when Pope John said, "My bags are packed. I am ready to leave." We are helping patients to pack their bags— each in his own individual way and making his own choices.'

It is not part of our purpose here to go into the various definitions of death—molecular, somatic, clinical, chemical, theological. The fact of death, for our purpose, is when the heart and breathing have stopped; although in certain circumstances it may be necessary to use an electro-encephalogram to monitor the activity of the brain to determine if there is any movement.

Where approaching death is not complicated by chemical intervention, or overt symptoms of the causative illness itself, the signs of dissolution are visible. The muscles of the face sag, there is a general failure of temperature, a cold dew of perspiration on the skin, a waxy paleness and a loss of transparency. The nostrils dilate, the eyes stare without seeing, the face and body twitches, the eyebrows elevate, the breathing is shallow and quick and ends with a distinctive gasp.

Fear of death is common to most, if not all, cultures. The dread is not so much about the process of dying—as has been noted by the Buddhists of Tibet, or the Muslims—as about the unknown that lies beyond death. Children speak quite freely about death. Adolescents tend to hide their true feelings by joking about death. Adults in the West view death as a taboo subject—especially in the presence of death—and use ambiguous expressions for it such as 'passing on', 'departing', 'breathing his last', 'leaving the body'.

Fear of death is the ultimate fear in life. Fear is the most insidious of addictions. Fear is bondage, and addiction means bondage. As the Apostle Peter declared: 'A man is a slave to whatever has mastered him.' Fear is not only a consequence of addictions, or even a cause of addictions, it is an addiction.

People become hooked on fear as an addiction. The gambler loves the sensation of fear involved in placing and losing his money. He does not care whether he wins or loses; it is the high from the fear he loves. Behind the gambler's sensation of excitement lies the source-impulse of fear, just as behind the alcoholic's or junkie's sensation of pleasure lies the source-impulse of the chemical substance.

Fear is the reason why horror films and novels are so popular. They are sought for the stimulus of fear they provide. The more outrageous the content the more satisfying the sensation.

Fear is cultivated as an excuse for not dealing with situations. Children use fear to avoid discipline. They plead fear of the dark to avoid going to sleep; fear of loneliness to avoid going to their room; fear of schoolmates to avoid going to school; fear of schoolteachers to avoid studies; fear of sports to avoid exercise; fear of accidents to avoid work. They grow up *enjoying* fear for the pleasure it provides. And parents are often quick to indulge them in these destructive practices that lead to later more serious conditions because of fears of their own.

Adults use fear to avoid facing up to responsibilities. Fear of losing an indulgent parent leads them to avoid marriage. Fear of the costs of bringing up children leads them to refuse to have any. Fear of what family and friends might say leads to restricting the number of children one or other spouse may want. Fear of neighbours leads to buying houses or providing education beyond the fiscal means. Fear keeps men and women in the same neighbourhood or the same house for most of their lives. Fear keeps many sick when they are well. Fear keeps many to their homes, to their rooms, even to their beds, when there is nothing physically wrong with them.

Fear is the most dominant experience in most people's lives. More people know fear than know love. People are prepared to work at cultivating fear when they are reluctant to cultivate love.

More homes are destroyed by fear than by any other experience. More divorces are caused by fear than any other cause. More murders are caused by fear than by hate.

Fear is Satan's greatest weapon in his war with God. The dark and formless evil that lies at the edge of consciousness in every fear-inducing circumstance—whether of child, or youth, or adult—is the presence of Satan, 'the Adversary'. His implacable intention in every circumstance of life is to distract from any thoughts of the reverential fear of God and its consequent commitment to obedience.

From the day we acknowledge the stated fear of our children, and indulge them in avoiding obedience to an order

because of fear of reaction from child or spouse or family, we
hand them over to the control of Satan. They *like* the state
which the blackmailing fear has produced on their behalf.
Like Satan himself they prefer, in the words of Milton, 'to
reign in hell rather than serve in heaven'. They come to
prefer the servitude of Satan to the demands of the discipline
of God. 'A man is a slave to whatever has mastered him.'
This is the 'wisdom not from above' spoken of by the Apostle
James, which is 'earthly, unspiritual and of the devil'.

To encourage people to indulge fear by accepting 'once
an alcoholic always an alcoholic', or 'once a junkie always a
junkie', is not to recognise 'God as we understand Him'. It is
to hand the individual over to a lifetime bondage to Satan.
The 'Power outside ourselves' is then not divine but demonic.
The mind is not transformed and renewed into new life; it is
deformed and consolidated into rigid infirmity.

In his book *Christianity and Fear*, Oscar Pfister has stated:

> The study of fear and compulsion-neuroses, and
> of their effects on religious and ethical life,
> opened my eyes to important complexes of facts
> and to the laws governing them.
>
> I began to understand the causal necessity
> leading to extreme religious eccentricities, as
> well as to valuable new developments; I saw how
> the same conditions and revolutionary laws lead
> to the outbreak of religious and non-religious
> hallucinations; I acquired a new psychological
> understanding for the various orthodoxies with
> their fear of the letter they failed to understand,
> and of ceremonial subtilties [sic] which occur in
> many religions, including the Christian; I
> appreciated the significance of mysticism,
> hallucinations, inspirations, speaking with
> tongues, and various other manifestations of
> piety, the origins of which had hitherto been
> completely mysterious . . .

I understood that a loss of love which occurs in non-religious compulsion-neurotics must inevitably, in the religious, be a great overemphasis on dogma, an overemphasis leading to the complete worship of dogma with the result that frequently, and perhaps in most cases, Christianity ceased to be a religion of love and became a religion of fear . . .

The biblical, loving, Father-God has made it perfectly clear: 'You did not receive a spirit that makes you a slave again to fear . . .' God did not give us 'a spirit of fear, but a spirit of *power*, of *love*, and of *self-discipline*'.

These are the three great steps to deliver us from all fears. Accepting LOVE as a gift from God, through the death of Jesus Christ on our behalf and its redemptive cleansing from all sins committed. Accepting POWER as a gift from God, through the resurrection of Jesus Christ from the dead; the same power to overcome everything. Accepting the discipline of a loving God, by presenting your body as a daily sacrifice of SELF-DISCIPLINE.

This, Paul said, is 'true worship'. He added: 'Do not conform any longer to the pattern of this world, but be transformed by the renewing of your mind. Then you will be able to test and approve what God's will is—his good, pleasing, and perfect will.'

This kind of commitment was demonstrated by Jesus Himself when faced by the greatest crisis of fear in His life. On the way to crucifixion at Calvary He spent the night in the Garden of Gethsemane with His disciples. He withdrew from them in order to pray to His Father for strength in the trial facing Him. He was not only being asked to give up His life at thirty-three years of age, blameless of any crime or fault, in a physically horrifying manner; He was about to face the undiluted opposition of Satan in a cosmic battle to settle the issue of control of death itself. Later, the writer of the epistle to the Hebrews would say:

> . . . It was fitting that God, for whom and
> through whom everything exists, should make
> the author of their salvation perfect through
> suffering . . . Since the children have flesh and
> blood he too shared in their humanity so that
> by his death he might destroy him who holds
> the power of death—that is, the devil—and
> free those who all their lives were held in
> slavery by their fear of death.

The greatest addiction is this fear of death: '. . . lives held
in slavery by their fear of death'. In order to be free of this
lifetime addiction it was necessary for someone to defeat 'him
who holds the power of death—that is, the devil'. That task
Jesus took on Himself in the battle to eliminate fear from
men and women everywhere. To accomplish this cosmic
victory Jesus had to master His own fears. We are told how
He did this.

In the Garden of Gethsemane, while His disciples slept,
Jesus entered into agonising prayer with His Father in heaven
over the form of death awaiting Him. It is said He prayed
three times. The following are the three responses to His
Father's will for Him:

One: 'My Father, if it is possible, may this cup be taken
from me. Yet not as I will, but as you will.'

Two: 'My Father, if it is not possible for this cup to be
taken away from me unless I drink it, may your will be done.'

Three: 'Shall I not drink the cup the Father has given
me?'

In coming to His final serene acceptance of His Father's
will for Him, Jesus passed through the utmost pressures of
fear, 'sweating like great drops of blood' as He agonised over
the consequences of 'being made sin by a holy God', of being
'forsaken by God'. But in His self-discipline of final sacrifice
He passed from the 'good will' of God in His first response: 'If
it be possible may this cup pass from me' to the 'pleasing will'
of God in His second response: 'If it is not possible for this

cup to be taken from me unless I drink it, may your will be done'; and, finally, to His confident assertion of the 'perfect will' of God in His third response: 'Shall I not drink the cup the Father has given me?'

In this way was 'the captain of our salvation made perfect through suffering'. He conquered fear, the ultimate fear of death, by a confident faith in the power of God to deliver Him from Satan and hell and carry Him triumphantly to heaven 'to make intercession for us'. By His perfect sacrifice in offering up Himself at God's command He came to know God's 'good, pleasing, perfect will'—and in the process was perfected in the suffering and made a perfect High Priest and Advocate in heaven for all sinners of all times.

This is the fear of God, the beginning and end of all wisdom. Absolute obedience to God out of absolute love for God. This is the ultimate Fear Factor without which no one will see God—or enter Paradise.

CHAPTER 6

The Nature of Fear

C.S. Lewis said of fear in *The Case for Christianity*:

> I am indeed far from agreeing with those who
> think all religious fear barbarous and degrading,
> and demand that it should be banished from
> the spiritual life. Perfect love, we know, casts
> out fear. But so do several other things—
> ignorance, alcohol, passion, presumption and
> stupidity. It is very desirable we should all
> advance to that perfection of love in which we
> shall fear no longer; but it is very undesirable
> that we should allow any inferior agent to cast
> out fear.

The workaholic is plagued by fear: fear from lack of
confidence in his or her performance within normal hours of
work patterns; fear of his or her output within the normal
parameters; fear of friends, or spouse, or family, or relatives, or
employer, or colleagues, if he or she should fall short of their
expectations; fear of the inner sense of inadequacy.

The 'superior civilisation' of the secular humanists in the
twentieth century, launched by the philosophers and
intellectuals of 'the Enlightenment' of the eighteenth
century, is ending in a *götterdämmerung* of fear just like its
predecessor, the French Revolution—begun with high hopes
and grandiose claims, but ending with terror and tyranny.

We have not yet reached terror and tyranny, but we are
well on the way. Pusillanimous politicians, and media and

academic pundits, can still be heard and read applauding the 'high standards of civilisation' of the twentieth century—while ignoring the soaring crime rates which hold the cities of their respective countries in thrall to a fear which imprisons their citizens in their homes after dark, and even there holds them terrified of break-ins, muggings, robberies, rapes and murder.

Fear is the dominating experience of all. Children fear their parents' divorce, adult sex battering and abuse, being sent away to school, bullying or discrimination. The youth of both sexes fear inadequacy, or rejection, or no careers, or no future (in the USA the peak age for committing a crime is now fifteen; and today almost one in four 13- to 15-year-olds commits an indictable crime). Adults fear unemployment, or insolvency, or demotion, or lack of recognition in politics or professions or social class.

There is fear of nuclear catastrophe; fear of nuclear waste dumping. There is fear of the consequences of accelerating atmospheric, stratospheric and environmental pollution. There is fear of war, fear of illness, fear of loneliness, fear of death.

Fear is a constant companion of all addicts, whether the addiction is chemical or behavioural: fear of external consequences, such as being found out by spouse, or parents, or relatives, or employers; or fear of internal consequences, such as overdosing, lung cancer, *delirium tremens*, incurable addiction or death.

This fear in addicts is either the cause of, or the product of, the equally predominant phenomenon of monomania, a characteristic feature of the addict. All chemical and behavioural addicts are self-centred, caring nothing for the consequences their addictions inflict on others—except, occasionally, for passing superficial and insincere expressions of regret for their selfish behaviour to suit their own interests. Their inability to deal with fear and self-love produces guilt and shame and self-loathing, and these in turn create new fears in an endless cycle.

The ancient sages, philosophers, and scholastics were

aware of the widespread prevalence of fear among humankind and gave a great deal of thought to its nature. Fear, Aristotle said, is a kind of sadness. St John Damascene declared fear to be an expression of the power of desire. St Thomas Aquinas concluded that, since fear is found in both sadness and desire and these were 'impulse emotions', fear is not 'a specific emotion'. He quoted St Augustine: 'A man who is not overcome by fear is neither overwhelmed by desire nor wounded by sickness, that is, sadness, nor shaken by bursts of empty delight.'

Fear is the most basic of all instincts. It did not exist in the Garden of Eden until Adam and Eve disobeyed God. Where perfect love is, there is no cause for fear. But love involves obedience. 'If you love me,' said Jesus, 'keep my commandments.' The intrusion of disobedience, as we have noted, precipitates fear.

When Adam and Eve disobeyed the command of God, regarding eating from the tree of the knowledge of good and evil, they went and hid themselves. When God asked Adam why, Adam said: '. . . I was afraid'. From that time on, Adam and Eve knew fear every day of their lives.

That fear came in three basic forms: fear of the known, fear of the unknown, and fear of God. *The fear of the known* they had already experienced when they clothed their bodies on their own initiative. 'Who told you you were naked?' God asked them. *The fear of the unknown* lay in what was waiting for them outside the Garden of Eden, with all of its potential physical terrors. *The fear of God* was in their self-chosen uncertain relationship with God; that third, numinous and wholesome, fear of God as their Creator, had been violated and fragmented by their first act of disobedience, by their easy seduction by the glittering, serpentine Satan, by their wilful yielding to the lust for forbidden knowledge. Now there was no solid ground of divine acceptance beneath their feet as they faced the rest of their lives, but rather a dark future under the judgement of God, and a tenuous relationship with God under His grace.

This divinely implanted dichotomy—fear of God as terror, and fear of God as reverence—as we have demonstrated earlier, is an essential part of the spiritual experience. Without the former there would be no individual compulsion to obedience; without the latter there would be no individual compulsion to worship. Obedience, says God, is more important than sacrifice, and worship is more essential than service. Fear of God keeps them in proper balance. When this fear of God was present the nation of Israel fulfilled their great destiny; when it was absent they went their own way to disaster and destruction.

The same was true of the New Testament church of God. At the launching at Pentecost it was recorded: 'And *fear came upon every soul*; and many wonders and signs were done by the apostles . . .' (Acts 2:43); '. . . *and great fear came upon all the church*, and upon as many as heard these things' (Acts 5:11). 'Then the churches had rest . . . *and walking in the fear of the Lord*, and in the comfort of the Holy Ghost, were multiplied . . .' (Acts 9:31). (our italics)

The 'fear of God', therefore, is an essential prerequisite for the individual believer and the corporate people of God at all times. The Apostle Paul said: 'Since, then, *we know the fear of the Lord*, we try to persuade men . . .' (our italics) Without the fear of God there can be no acceptable or proper relationship between the creature and the Creator.

The first-century philosopher Seneca, in his *Epistles*, said: 'The trip doesn't exist that can set you beyond the reach of cravings, fits of temper, or fears. If it did, the human race would be off there in a body.'

Two thousand years later the human race is still seeking a 'trip' that will take them beyond cravings, temper and fears, only now the experience they seek is not a distant and physical voyage but an inward and chemical retreat. The 'Fear Factor', however, is the same. Joseph Conrad, in his *Tales of Unrest*, writes: 'A man may destroy everything within himself, love and hate and belief, and even doubt; but as long as he clings to life he cannot destroy fear.'

Albert Camus, in *The Fall*, said that this period of history was 'the century of fear', in comparison with the seventeenth century as the age of mathematics, the eighteenth as the age of the physical sciences, and the nineteenth as that of biology; adding, 'Moreover, although fear itself cannot be considered a science, it is certainly a technique.'

Pascal in his *Pensées* defined the two types of fear: 'There is a *virtuous fear* which is the effect of faith, and a *vicious fear* which is the product of doubt and distrust. The former leads to hope as relying on God, in whom we believe; the latter inclines to despair, or not relying on God, in whom we do not believe. Persons of the one character fear to lose God; those of the other character fear to find Him.'

What Blaise Pascal called 'vicious fear' was the first alien emotion experienced by our first parents, Adam and Eve, in the Garden of Eden after they had defied the commands of God. Until then their primary emotion had been love— towards each other, towards creation, and towards God—and 'virtuous fear'. Afterwards they knew the vicious 'fear that is stronger than love' in the words of Pliny the Second. With the coming of the serpentine Satan, and the knowledge of evil, they knew destructive fear—and they hid themselves. When God asked them why they hid themselves, they replied, 'We were afraid.'

According to Aristotle fear is the 'pain arising from the anticipation of evil'. The modern Oxford Dictionary defines it: '. . . alarm, painful emotion caused by impending danger or evil'. But this is just 'secular' or profane fear, even when applied to a spirit being; what an anonymous writer described as:

> They that worship God merely from fear
> Would worship the devil too, if he appear.

'Sacred', or spiritual, fear has a wider and deeper meaning, which neither of these definitions comprehend. Sacred, or virtuous, fear rises above the anticipation of pain or danger or evil into a spiritual realm and relationship which precipitates the emotion of awe and reverence and worship. There is no room for alarm, or anxiety, or dread, or terror, in that experience because the knowledge of the accepting presence of God is the dominating element.

George's first experience of the 'fear of the spirit world' occurred shortly after he arrived in Tibet. He and his colleague, Geoff Bull, had moved out of the China Inland Mission compound into a house of their own. One night George heard a crash from Geoff's bedroom, and when he went through to see what had happened he found Geoff lying on the floor semi-conscious and bewildered. Geoff's explanation was that he had some sort of nightmare, with a deep impression 'of impending evil'. This happened a few times, and then one night when George rushed through to Geoff's room he found him standing on the window ledge about to jump out, under the influence of the same 'evil' impulse. They decided that there must be some inexplicable 'demonic' element in the circumstances, and they went round the house exorcising the demon influence by prayer. It disappeared, although a similar experience happened to George too, later, in different circumstances.

This was the start of George's introduction into the tantric practices of Tibetan Buddhism, which occupied him for several years after he left Tibet and its borders. As his ability in the Tibetan language, and his knowledge of the tantric practices, increased, George found a unique dichotomy in Tibetan religious practices, both in homes and temples. In addition to the standard idols of Buddha and his disciples in homes and temples and monasteries, there was always an annexe in which there were other black-faced or blue-faced idols with savage expressions. The latter were said to be the 'guardian deities', and the offerings before them were always better than the offerings before the orthodox Buddhist idols.

After a time it became apparent to George that the prayers addressed to these guardian deities were also different in expression. When he found a Tibetan lama who was able to teach him what was happening, he was informed that the orthodox Buddhist idols were the 'benevolent' deities, whose disposition was to help the human race; the other dark-faced 'guardian deities' were 'malevolent', and their mission was to destroy the human race. Therefore, in their prayers to the different deities the Tibetans used the equivalent of the term 'placate' when addressing the benevolent idols, and the term 'solicit' when they addressed the malevolent idols; and this difference in approach was also reflected in their offerings— an example of Pascal's 'virtuous' and 'vicious' fears.

For a time George worked with Prince Peter of Greece in the filming of a Tibetan *chod-gyad*, or tantric 'oracle' medium, who was able to be possessed by nine different 'deities' in the Tibetan pantheon. They filmed and interviewed him before, during and after the various ceremonies. It was a characteristic feature of the 'possession' sessions that the Tibetan medium was in considerable psychophysical distress as he emerged, and he took some time to recover. It was accepted by the participants that this psychophysical distress was a common experience of all mediums, and that it was a downward spiral into eventual mental imbalance and death.

In one of the discussions George had contributed the Christian viewpoint of possession as Jesus taught it; namely, that the Spirit of Christ in the believer was greater than the spirit of Satan. Prince Peter wanted to conduct an experiment on film to demonstrate the phenomenon, but George refused on the grounds that 'possession' in the Bible was a dangerous and serious violation of God's commands. However, a few days later the *chod-gyad* came to visit George on his own, and asked to be 'delivered' from the destructive deities who possessed him, as he was already on an accelerating downward path and was deeply afraid. George told him that he could have the malevolent 'deities' cast out, but it would involve an equally personal commitment to Jesus Christ as Lord as he had given to the demonic spirits. He was reluctant to take this step, and some months later he was reported to have committed suicide.

George's studies in demonism ended when he found himself being irresistibly drawn into a deeper Faust-like desire for personal experimentation with the spirit world. One night, some time after we were married, and after he had spent several hours studying medieval occultism in the British Museum Library, he was 'attacked' again in the middle of the night and Meg, too, was conscious of that overwhelming presence of evil in the room. George stopped his occultic studies immediately, and did not return to them for several years.

The distinction between fear and anxiety is clearly stated in both Old and New Testaments. The 'fear of God' was to be the basic emotion of the children of Israel in their destined relationship with God. He chose them, He said, because He loved them, not because they were lovable, or special in themselves, and He demanded that they fear Him at all times. In one of the many places where Moses makes this clear he said:

> The Lord said to me,'Gather the people together, and I will make them hear my words, *that they may learn to fear me all the days that they shall live upon the earth, and that they may teach their children* . . . O that their hearts would be inclined to fear me and keep all my commands always, *so that it might go well with them and their children forever* . . .' (our italics)

This was 'virtuous fear'. If the children of Israel as the chosen people of God kept this fear of God they would never need fear what any man or nation could do to them, for God would be with them at all times. In fact, the fear of God that was upon them, God said, would make all other peoples of all nations be in fear and dread of them. But if they forgot this fear of God, then they would know all aspects of fear— 'vicious fear'—in every department of their lives. God assured them:

Among the nations you will find *no repose, no resting place* for the sole of your foot. There the Lord will give you *an anxious mind, eyes weary with longing*, and *a despairing heart*. You will live *in constant suspense, filled with dread* both night and day, *never sure of your life*. In the morning you will say, 'If only it were evening!' and in the evening 'If only it were morning!'—*because of the terror* that will fill your hearts and the sights that your eyes will see. (our italics)

The purpose of the Creator for His creatures, then, was that in cultivating a virtuous fear of God, which would lead them into 'keeping His commands always', they need never know the vicious fears which are the consequences of disobedience. Anxiety, said God, would be a punishment for not exercising a positive and virtuous fear towards their Creator. Anxiety was something that God sent in response to disobedience—'The Lord will give you an anxious mind, etc.', as quoted above—and which could be easily removed by exercising obedience, prayer and gratitude. The Apostle Paul described it when writing to the church in Philippi: '*Do not be anxious about anything*, but in everything, by prayer and petition, with thanksgiving, present your requests to God.' (our italics)

It can therefore be assumed that where there are signs of vicious fear in any believer there is a lack of faith in God's words, and lack of conformity to God's commands. Where fears or anxieties are present in any believer it can be equally assumed that there is a lack of virtuous fear of God.

If we paraphrase Camus, it might be said that, from the Christian point of view, the seventeenth century was 'the age of justification by faith', the eighteenth was 'the age of sanctification of life', the nineteenth was 'the age of judgement hereafter', and the twentieth century is 'the age of God-rejection'. There has probably never been such a time of flagrant ignoring or defying of the commands of God. Before the printing of the Scriptures there was little opportunity for large-scale outright obedience or disobedience of God; but with the mass printing and distribution of the Bible world-wide there is no longer any excuse for all the people of God—both Jews and Christians—not to know and observe all that God requires of them.

Luther, Calvin, Wesley, Finney, Edwards, Moody, Graham, have all called on the people of God to hear and obey what God's purposes are for them in their generation. What is happening in the twentieth century among Christians is what has happened in the past millennia when professing children of God kept God's commands with their lips but their hearts and lives were far from Him. They 'have a form of godliness, but deny the power'. Like the Jews in their defiance of God and decline from their divine destiny between the times of David and Jesus, they produce countless new ideas, new forms of religion, proliferating ecclesiastics, multiplicity of literary works—and demonstrable evidence that God is no longer in their midst. Despite all the sacrifices and religious services, while Jesus lived among His fellow Jews, it was apparent to all that the Temple had no Ark, no Shekinah and no God. Yet everybody acted as if they were still there! There was no fear of God.

Nineteen centuries after communicating directly with His creatures, on a basis of total obedience to His spoken commands, it is now being made to appear as if God has opted out of personally directing any of His divine purposes on earth, and we are being asked to believe that He has left it to the professional religionists to operate on His behalf and just keep us informed when they get around to it in their rota of sermons. The theologians among them would have us accept that they are authorised interpreters of the mind of God, some of the more sanctimonious among them claiming immodestly to have the exclusive help of the Holy Spirit in this enlightenment.

The problem with this claimed privileged association is at least twofold: one, that these ecclesiastics appear to be inhibited from asserting, as all God's true spokesmen in the past did, 'Thus says the Lord' (they might well say, 'Thus says the Scriptures', another matter of personal interpretation altogether, as Satan demonstrated to Jesus); and, two, they lack evidence of the awesome fear of God that comes from a knowledge of and association with Him.

Stop reading right there, and ask yourself: when did I last see a Christian of any note who had either of these two necessary attributes? They lack the Fear Factor.

Nor is this addressed only to those who occupy positions of ecclesiastical responsibility, delegated to them from whatever seminary 'ordained' them. It is true in any church at any time. Do people gather in your church with any sign of expectation that they are going into the presence of Almighty God? Is the meeting-place of any kind— household, hall, church, chapel, cathedral—quiet and hushed in reverence, in awe, in *fear*? What are the signs that the God of Abraham, Isaac and Jacob, the God of Moses and Samuel and David and Elijah, the God of John and Jesus and Paul, is present?

Is it not true that there are few, if any, signs evident? The members meet outside and inside as if it were a theatre, or club, or football match. Views about the weather, children, families, friends, even employment—or the match—are exchanged. Inside, either loud-voiced or low-voiced conversation is carried on, and social engagements are fixed. Young unmarried or newly marrieds hold hands, encircle waists, gaze and smile, during the hymns of worship or speaker's address. Mothers open large handbags and take out comics or colouring books to occupy the children's attention. As they file out there is a mounting crescendo of social chit-chat.

Are You listening, God? Are You watching, God? Do

You not really care, God? What kind of God are You now in the twentieth century? Is this what You anticipated with the departure of Your Son, the coming of the Holy Spirit, and the death of the apostles? Are You content to sit up there and let Your representatives on earth behave in this fashion without any sign of rebuke, after spending two millennia and providing two Testaments trying to educate the world about what kind of jealous, majestic and mighty God You are? Is the Fear Factor not important any more?

George was brought up in Scotland among Christians known as 'Brethren'. After some years as a Sunday School and Bible Class teacher, he spent some time as an open-air preacher, and then was asked to preach at one of the regular inside meetings of a prominent neighbouring church. He was twenty-one years of age at the time, and the Brethren in Central Scotland were usually reluctant to have any 'young man' preach or teach before thirty, as that was the age when John the Baptist and Jesus 'entered into public ministry'. It was a great honour, therefore, for George to be asked to speak at one of the large meetings. It was also a demanding experience, for the older members often came to these meetings with two or more different versions of the Bible, and sometimes with a Greek and Hebrew lexicon!

The chairman for the meeting was an old family friend, Bob Easson, well-known throughout Scotland, respected and feared. After he had opened the meeting with hymns and prayer he introduced George and sat down on the platform behind him. George walked to the lectern, spread out his Bible, and, to give an impression of calmness he did not feel, he put his hands in his jacket pockets. He took a deep breath to begin, when Mr Easson's voice behind him said clearly, 'Take your hands out of your pockets, you're in the presence of the Lord.' That was forty-five years ago and George never stands up to speak anywhere, anytime, but he still hears those words ringing in his ears. The Fear Factor.

Henry Ward Beecher wrote: 'God planted fear in the soul as truly as He planted hope or courage. It is a kind of bell or gong which rings the mind into quick life and avoidance on the approach of danger. It is the soul's signal for rallying.'

In order to face the fact of death with equanimity, with glad acceptance as an entrance to Paradise, it is necessary to first conquer fear.

CHAPTER 7

The Conquest of Fear

*I*n his book, *The Second Sin*, Thomas Szasz, writes:

> Powerful addictions . . . are actually both very difficult and very easy to overcome. Some people struggle vainly against such a habit for decades; others 'decide' to stop and are done with it; and sometimes those who have long struggled in vain manage to rid themselves of the habit. How can we account for this? Not only is the pharmacology of the so-called addictive substance irrelevant to this riddle, but so is the personality of the so-called addict. What is relevant is whether the 'addiction' is or is not part of an internally significant dramatic production in which the 'patient-victim' is the star. So long as it is, the person will find it difficult or impossible to give up the habit whereas, once he has decided to close down this play and leave the stage, he will find the grip of the habit broken and will 'cure' himself of the 'addiction' with surprising ease.

But this act of surrender—to family, relatives, friends, society, doctor or God—in order to overcome the fundamental 'Fear Factor' is an enormous and, to many, an impossible hurdle. The Third Step of Alcoholics Anonymous' Twelve Steps is this act of surrender: 'We made a decision to turn our will and life over to the care of God as we understand Him.' This Third Step Alcoholics Anonymous often describe as 'letting go and letting God'.

Unfortunately, it is both an illusion and solution as many

Alcoholics Anonymous members will testify. It is an illusion as presented '. . . to turn our will and life over to God as we understand Him'. For many, this is a prescription to create a God in their own image; to individually define his or her own personal religion; to make their own 'god-in-a-box'. It is like saying that the individual is willing to let his legs move, but wants God to catch the bus or taxi for him. The God they create is a manipulated Deity suiting their own convenience and inclination.

True surrender involves *choosing* God, not *making* God; of being formed according to this God's will, and not forming God according to one's own decisions and desires. Otherwise, it is the superstitious idolatry of the twentieth-century pagans: making a god of ideas and opinions, instead of the former gold or silver or wood.

This kind of 'individualised religion' is an addiction in itself—yet another form of behavioural addiction, to add to workaholism (addiction to performance); or mammonism (addiction to making money); or sportaholism (addiction to excitement); or gambling (addiction to risk-taking); or ecclesiasticism (addiction to church activities) and the other ritualistic obsessional indulgences.

The practice of religion can be an obsessive addiction, when it is uncritically accepted, unteachably practised, and bigotedly believed. Kierkegaard, the Danish philosopher-theologian, declared that the most malignant form of religious addiction arose from 'perfectionistic expectations of our own selves'; these religious addicts, he said, are 'people who get drunk on infinitude'. The true 'knight of faith', he maintained, has one foot in the finite, and one in the infinite. He or she sees things as they are, as well as how they should be and will be.

Throughout his life Martin Luther admitted he suffered from fear. His strict upbringing and education involved innumerable severe beatings. It was the fear of death induced by lightning striking close to him which persuaded him to vow to become a monk. He went into a monastery because of fear of the judgements of God and hoping to find peace. He confessed that he always celebrated Mass 'with the utmost terror'.

It was only when Luther understood and accepted the Scriptural teaching of justification by faith—the acceptance by an individual of God's offer of imputed righteousness through the sacrifice of Christ on the cross—that he was delivered from his chronic fears. The exercise of faith in this demonstration of the love of God, and of the love of Christ, was a recurrent experience which provided alleviation from fear and an inner security and joy that his previous rigorous and ritualistic monasticism had failed to give him.

In the twentieth century Sigmund Freud, the father of psychoanalysis, devoted himself to a study of fear. He also came to the conclusion that it was closely related to love. But there was a world of difference between Freud's concept of love as sex-drive, *libido*, and Jesus' love as sacrificial affection, *agape*. Freud derived certain pathological manifestations of fear, which he described as genuinely neurotic, from inhibitions of sexuality, inhibitions of the love life, taken as an impulsive activity. Fear, he argued, is the reaction of the ego to the internal danger of a threatening inhibition; the punishment of infantile Oedipus desires, which are interpreted not only as prohibited desires for love but also as hate, and consequently as guilt, causing the consciousness to become aware that punishment is threatening.

What can be agreed from both the biblical and modern psychological definitions of fear is that the two chief causes of fear are an interference with the impulse towards love in general, and a sense of guilt in particular. This includes the suppressions and repressions of spiritual love as well as self-love, for whatever reasons.

Fear can be caused by an excess as well as a deficiency of love. It can be experienced in the indulged as well as the deprived, for the simple reason that the claims of the indulged for love expand until they become impossible of fulfilment.

Again, an excessive restriction on the impulse towards freedom—what the gloomy existential Danish philosopher-theologian, Kierkegaard, described as 'liberty in bonds'—also induces a predisposition to fear. Self-preservation, deprivation, distress of certain kinds, contribute to the experience of fear.

But what is important to keep in mind is that fear is induced in these and other circumstances only when the individual has failed to find an adequate compensation for the object denied him or her. The very existence of fear implies an absence of adequate love. The predisposition to fear implies a lack of appropriate compensatory emotional and spiritual mechanisms to deal with the threatening impulses or inhibitions. The stronger the predisposition to fear the more likely it is that the precipitating factor will be insignificant. For example, to certain individuals a spider, or mouse, or small dog, induce fear while a larger animal, or even person, will not.

Fear and love are both concerned with the agreeable or disagreeable source-impulses; they may shrink from something that is disagreeable, such as a snake; but also from something that is agreeable but can inflict harm, such as a horse.

This is an important observation, for it explains why people 'fear God'—because He is able to inflict a spiritual or physical punishment as well as bestow unmerited love. It also explains why there is so much confusion regarding a proper fear of God: with spiritual love God can be perceived as an agreeable source-impulse evoking reverential and joyful worship; but with self-love—and its accompanying sense of guilt, a derivative of fear—God is perceived as a disagreeable source-impulse, and this invokes fear as dread, hate and rejection.

Jesus did not provide those who followed Him and His teachings freedom from fear. On the contrary, He asserted they would be hated as He was hated, that so long as they were in the world they would have tribulations ('fear'); but,

He said to them, 'Be not afraid . . . be of good cheer . . . I have overcome . . . these things I have spoken to you that in me you may have peace.' The true inheritance of the follower of Jesus Christ is joy, peace and love—intimations on earth of the Paradise waiting in heaven. The repression and suppression of fear was the individual responsibility of every follower of Jesus. Time after time when He was with them He rebuked them for their fears as a sign of their lack of faith.

'Fear,' said Augustine, 'leads to the love of charity. Without any doubt there is no other cause of fear than that we should lose what we have, after having obtained it, or should not obtain it when we hope to.'

The Apostle Paul of Tarsus pointed out to the Christians in the Roman church of his time: 'You did not receive the spirit of bondage again to fear, but you received the spirit of adoption by whom we cry out, "Abba, Father".'

Paul was making two very important statements: firstly, he was emphasising the freedom from fear of all those who accepted God's gift of love and salvation through Jesus Christ; and secondly, he was emphasising the radical transformation in status and relationship of the Christian adopted into the family of God.

Paul elaborated on this when he wrote to the young Timothy: 'For God [our Father] has not given us a spirit of fear, but of power and love and a sound mind.'

Power, love and a sound mind—or 'self-discipline'. These are a stated gift of God in opposition to the experience of fear. Any addiction treatment process which speaks of 'God as we understand Him', and then condones aspects of fear— such as negative possibilities of relapse, or of indulgence, for whatever reasons—has an inadequate God, and certainly does not have a Judaeo-Christian God, however individuals may 'understand Him'.

In the Old Testament the relationship between God as Creator and His creatures, and God as Redeemer and His children, was based on a combination of love and fear: 'You shall love the Lord your God with all your heart': 'You shall fear the Lord your God and serve Him only.' The tragedy of the children of Israel was that they refused to do both. It was left to Jesus to demonstrate the divine ideal.

All of the thoughts, words and acts of Jesus flowed from the fundamental love which He experienced within Himself as the supreme revelation, certitude and imperative of God. He declared with total and unchallengeable confidence: 'He that has seen me has seen the Father.' And the Apostle John said: 'By this shall all men know love, because he laid down his life for us.'

The love that Jesus demonstrated was wholly different from the Platonic *eros* or the Stoic love of mankind of his time. It was not just an abstract proposition, for in its essence, impulse and direction it resulted in kindness, righteousness, justice and truth to their fullest extent. It was because of love, and not of fear, that Jesus kept God's laws, and He imposed the same obligation on all who desired to follow Him in obedience to God. He said to His followers just before His death:

> As the Father has loved me, so have I loved you. Now remain in my love. If you obey my commands, you will remain in my love, just as I have obeyed my Father's commands and remain in his love. I have told you this so that my joy may be in you and that your joy may be complete (John 15:9–11).

It was the imbalance in their understanding of the divine requirements of love and fear that led to the insubordination of the children of Israel throughout the Old Testament. And it was the proper balance in His understanding of the divine requirements of love and fear that characterised the life and teachings of Jesus. For Jesus, to love God meant the total submission to the written commands of God in the Scriptures and to the spoken will of God in His daily life.

Jesus' submission to the will of His Father was not just a deterministic bondage, as it would have been if activated only by fear as dread of the judgement of God. It had another dimension that lifted it above and beyond fear as dread, the element of joy: 'I *delight* to do your will, O God', He could say; '. . . who, for the *joy* that was set before him, endured the cross . . .' This joy was inspired by a true understanding of the Father's love, and it evoked fear of God as reverential awe.

The most significant characteristic of love, therefore, is a willing devotion and an associated indescribable pleasure of being attracted towards the object of love. Obedience to the desires and commands of the loved one are only the consequences of this joyful response. Out of this arises a synthesis of love and reverence for God, and of love and devotion to humankind, which eliminates deterministic bondage.

For Jesus, the touchstone of all obedience was a consciousness of God's love behind the divine commands—just as it was for the Psalmist—and the consequence of this was that, in the direst of circumstances, there was no fear; only a joyous realisation of the presence and perfect will of God. Where there was love of God there was no room for fear of men.

This is the fear of God, the beginning and end of all wisdom. Absolute obedience to God out of absolute love for God. This is the ultimate Fear Factor without which no one will see God—or enter Paradise. The Scriptural God, the God of both the Old and New Testaments, requires only that His creatures 'fear God' on a basis of love and understanding, and then He promises the removal of all other fears, and the replacement with paradisal joys.

It is unfortunate that twentieth-century followers of Jesus Christ should, on the occasion of deaths in their families, adopt all the customs of unbelieving pagans in their public demonstrations of grief, bewilderment and bereavement. They even derive support for their unscriptural conduct from Jesus at the grave of Lazarus when it is said: 'When Jesus saw her [Mary] weeping, and the Jews who had come along with her also weeping, he was deeply moved in spirit and troubled ... Jesus wept.'

But it is obvious from the context of the incident, and from Jesus' own words at the time, that He was trying to get them to understand the true significance of the resurrection from the dead. How could He, who was about to raise Lazarus in a demonstration of His power over death, weep at the prospect of death? It is ludicrous. No, Jesus was weeping at the demonstrations of unnecessary grief being experienced by Mary and the other so-called believers in resurrection. If they had only believed Him, they had the Lord of Eternal Life beside them, and paradisal joy should have been their experience—and public witness.

Certainly, the professional religionists were aware of the significance of what Jesus had done. They said: 'If we let him go on like this everyone will believe in him ... So from that time on they plotted to take his life.' They, too, were absurd in their response; for they decided to put to death the person who had just demonstrated that He had power over death.

The true response of Christians in the twentieth century to the presence of death should be paradisal joy and not paralysing grief. The hymn they sing should be 'When the Saints Go Marching In' (preferably played by a rousing New Orleans jazz band!) and not the dolorous 'When This Passing World is Done' in oppressive gloom. Christians should be teaching the world the art of dying.

CHAPTER 8

The Art of Dying

*I*t was the ancient Greek philosopher Epicurus, teaching that the chief purpose of humankind was to obtain happiness in this life because there is no life after death, who said: 'The art of living and the art of dying are one.'

It was not Cain, who first brought death on earth by murdering his brother Abel, who first brought the art of living and dying according to the good pleasure of the Creator; but Abraham, the father of the nation of Israel much later.

The favourite work of the philosopher Søren Kierkegaard, and one that he wished to be remembered for by posterity, was entitled *Fear and Trembling*. It is a study of Abraham, and he wrote of it: 'Once I am dead then *Fear and Trembling* alone will give me the name of an immortal author. Then it will be read . . . and people will almost shudder at the frightful pathos of the book . . .'

Isaac, Abraham's divinely promised son, was about twenty years old when God said to Abraham: 'Take your son, your only son, Isaac, whom you love, and go to the region of Moriah. Sacrifice him there as a burnt offering on one of the mountains I will tell you about.'

Incredibly, there is no record that Abraham ever argued with God, or even expressed bewilderment. The Scriptures continue: 'Early the next morning Abraham saddled his donkey . . .' It was that phrase which so moved Kierkegaard: 'Early the next morning'. It even appeared as if Abraham actually welcomed the opportunity to obey God's command by getting up early to begin the three-day journey to the appointed place of sacrifice. What must have been his thoughts during those three days? When Isaac asked him about the animal for sacrifice in all the preparations being made, Abraham simply said that God would provide it in His own time.

At the appointed mountain of sacrifice the hundred-and-twenty-year-old Abraham somehow persuaded the twenty-year-old Isaac to place himself, and be bound, on the altar as a sacrifice, in obedience to the command of God. He picked up the sacrificial knife and, as he raised it above his head to slay his only son, God's appointed heir, a voice from heaven said to him:

> Do not lay a hand on the boy. Do not do anything to him. *NOW I know that you fear God, because you have not withheld from me your son, your only son.* (our italics)

Put another way, the incident might be interpreted that, until Abraham raised the knife above Isaac, he was still a man of immense faith, believing right up to that point that God would somehow miraculously intervene to spare Isaac. But there came a time when, in Abraham's mind, the awful truth dawned that God was not going to intervene, that God really wanted him to kill Isaac, and as the realisation dawned he knew he had an inadequate apprehension of God. He knew his faith was not enough to encompass the kind of God he had experienced until then. A thousand questions clamoured to be answered in that seemingly eternal moment, with the eyes of his trusting, doomed son fastened on him.

What about God's purposes regarding Isaac? What about the destiny of the divine programme? Was he going to have to wait another twenty years for a successor to Isaac? Had he truly heard God aright? Was God as unreliable as all the other gods? With the one stroke of the knife he was not only going to be set back fifty years, he was cast into a world without hope or faith. Unless . . .

The voice from heaven stopped the downstroke of the

blade: 'NOW I know that you fear God . . .'. At that point in time, when Abraham decided to trust the God he knew, even at the cost of destroying his son and his life's work and expectations—when God saw the decision made in Abraham's mind: 'NOW I know'—Abraham demonstrated that he had a proper fear of God: '. . . because you have not withheld from me your son, your only son'.

Once Abraham had shown that appropriate fear of God then the consequences of his faith followed naturally. The voice from heaven spoke to him again:

> Because you have done this, and have not withheld your son, your only son, I will surely bless you and make your descendants as numerous as the stars in the sky and as the sand on the seashore. Your descendants will take possession of the cities of their enemies, and through your offspring all the nations of the earth will be blessed, *because you have obeyed me.* (our italics)

Yet, take note. It was Isaac, not Abraham, who knew God as 'Fear'. At this unique point in human history, when God was affirming to Abraham the historical destiny of the people of Israel as those chosen to be His divine instrument on earth, *and through whom all nations of the world would be blessed,* it was because Abraham had a proper fear of God. It was this fear that led him to obey the command of God, and it was this fear that brought the Jews their unique destiny.

It was even more than this. God was establishing through Abraham, and his unique example of fear of God, the criterion by which every believer—Jew and Gentile—would be judged. It would be the symbol of that later sacrifice on the cross by Jesus: the father requiring the sacrifice of the son in the fear of, and obedience to, God. It was an unforgettable demonstration of both the Art of Living and the Art of Dying.

But there was still an even more important aspect to the
incident. It was the beginning of the unfolding revelation of
the character of God as represented in His Name. God
revealed Himself first to Abraham as El Shaddai ('Almighty
God': Gen.17:1), and as 'Shield of Abraham' (Gen. 15:1).
But it was on Mount Moriah, where Isaac was the willing
offering, that God revealed Himself uniquely in the divine
name of 'Fear of Isaac'.

Without Isaac's willing cooperation the aged Abraham
could never have forced him onto the altar and bound him.
Isaac feared to be the sacrifice, but if that was what God
wanted from him he freely offered himself. It was for this that
God uniquely honoured him in one of His titles. Of the three
Patriarchs of Israel whom God later linked together as sharers
of the divine covenant and promises—'the God of Abraham,
Isaac and Jacob'—it was only Isaac who knew Him as 'Fear'.
Abraham knew Him by the divine Name of 'Shield of
Abraham', and Jacob as 'Mighty One of Jacob' (Gen. 49:24);
but Isaac knew Him as 'Fear of Isaac'.

Twice Jacob, one of Isaac's sons, used this title in the
Scriptures: once, when he said, 'If the God of my father, the
God of Abraham, and *the Fear of Isaac*, had not been with me,
you would surely have sent me away empty-handed' (Gen.
31:42, our italics); and the second time, when he said, 'May
the God of Abraham and the God of Nahor, the God of their
father, judge between us. So Jacob took an oath in the name
of *the Fear of his father Isaac*' (Gen. 31:53, our italics).

Why would this name be revealed only to Isaac? Of all
the Patriarchs of Israel Isaac was the least memorable, so far
as any distinctive events in his life are concerned. Only two
unusual events are recorded: his marriage to Rebekah, and
being deceived by Rebekah and Jacob on his deathbed. So,
why 'the Fear of Isaac'?

We suggest it was because of that incident on the Mount
of Sacrifice. To Abraham, the father, it was an act of faith in

God; but to Isaac, the son, it was an act of fear of God. Should God require Isaac's death Abraham's faith could be realised by the birth of another son; but it meant the loss of everything for Isaac. From the time he left his parents' home Isaac knew, or at least suspected, he was to be the offering; that his parents' God required an obedience that transcended all human parameters. The God who was 'the Shield of Abraham' required from Isaac not only a filial submission to parental authority, but a cooperative and total self-sacrifice even unto death. Isaac had learned the Art of Dying.

The problem for an individual living in the twentieth century is that while he or she is prepared to devote an inordinate amount of time to acquiring the art of living well, they have lost the ability or commitment to learn how to die well.

The secret of dying well lies in the nature of the beliefs held by the dying person. Tibetans from the East Tibet province of Kham are descendants of the fearsome Genghis Khan tribesmen, and are famous warriors. Later, they became Buddhists, and over the centuries they have devoted themselves to the art of dying as outlined in their *Tibetan Book of the Dead*. From this they have learned to face death not only calmly but 'clearmindedly and heroically'; and they are contemptuous of anyone who has not mastered the process. But it takes time and application.

In his introduction to his translation of *The Tibetan Book of the Dead* Dr W. Y. Evans-Wentz says:

> . . . the dying should face death . . . with an intellect rightly trained and rightly directed, mentally transcending if need be, bodily suffering and infirmities, as they would be able to do had they practised efficiently during their active lifetime the Art of Living, and, when about to die, the Art of Dying . . . But in the

Occident, where the Art of Dying is little known and rarely practised, there is, contrastingly, the common unwillingness to die, which as the *Bardo* ritual suggests, produces unfavourable results.

Dr Evans-Wentz goes on to say:

Buddhists and Hindus alike believe that the last thought at the moment of death determines the character of the next incarnation. As the *Bardo Thodol* teaches . . . the thought-process of a dying person should be rightly directed, preferably by the dying person if he or she has been initiated or psychically trained to meet death, or, otherwise, by a guru or a friend or relative versed in the science of death . . . Our past thinking has determined our present status, and our present thinking will determine our future status; for man is what man thinks . . .

In her book, *Death and Dying*, Dr Elizabeth Kubler-Ross describes a characteristic fivefold process in the act of dying: denial, anger, bargaining, depression and acceptance. Upon hearing the verdict of death the first reaction of the individual concerned is 'No, not me.' Then comes the anger, 'Why me?'—against the doctor, life, fate, God. The third stage involves bargaining: 'Yes me, but . . . just give me a few more years until my children are older, etc.' The fourth stage is depression, when the individual says in gloomy resignation, 'If it must be me, then so be it'—but there is resentment, grief, fear. The fifth stage is acceptance, when the individual faces the inevitability of death with apathy at the least, and equanimity at the best.

All of these characteristics of the presence of dying can be found in the Scriptures. For example, when King David of Israel committed adultery with Bathsheba, and a child was born of the union, it was the judgement of God that the child would die (2 Samuel 12:11–20). David's first reaction was denial ('David fasted and went in and lay all night upon the ground'). His second reaction was anger ('the servants were afraid to tell him that the child was dead . . . "He may do something desperate" ') Then David bargained ('David pleaded with God for the child'). Then he was depressed ('he would not rise, nor did he eat food'). Finally, David accepted the inevitable ('David arose from the ground, washed and anointed himself . . . went into the house of God and worshipped').

In the New Testament the same order of reactions can be seen in the family of Martha and Mary with the fact of the death of Lazarus. A programmed scheme of ameliorative responses to counter those five characteristics can be developed, as demonstrated by Dr Kubler-Ross. A far better programme can be presented from the Scriptures, as we indicate in this book.

In both the instances quoted above—of David and the child, and Jesus and Lazarus—the Scriptural means of overcoming the fact of death was by acknowledging the belief in resurrection. David said: 'He shall not come to me, but I shall go to him.' And Jesus said to Martha, Mary and the others: ' Did I not tell you that if you believed (in resurrection) you would see the glory of God?' Note: he did *not* say they would 'see Lazarus'—although they did—but 'see the glory of God'.

But obviously it is better for the individual *not* to wait until the moment of death to concentrate the mind on an appropriate spiritual thought. Deathbed conversions are notoriously unreliable in both time and content. Then again, the best-laid schemes could be thwarted by the disease causing the death. Shakespeare's words in the mouth of the contemptuous Cassius regarding Caesar are apposite in this regard:

> He had a fever when he was in Spain,
> And when the fit was on him, I did mark

How he did shake. 'Tis true, this god did shake;
His coward lips did from their colour fly;
And that same eye, whose bend doth awe the
    world,
Did lose his lustre! I did hear him groan;
Ay! and that tongue of his, that bade the
    Romans
Mark him, and write his speeches in their
    books—
Alas! it cried, Give me some drink, Titinius,
As a sick girl.

In the words of La Rochefoucauld: 'One can no more look steadily at death than at the sun.' And it is said that Gertrude Stein told Ernest Hemingway he ceased to be a great writer when he became obsessed with sex and death. So death and its terrors must be viewed in proportion to all other aspects of life, always remembering that 'in the midst of life we are in death'.

It was Solomon the Wise—who devoted his life to the Art of Living, and described some of his conclusions in the books of Proverbs, Ecclesiastes and Song of Solomon—who gives one of the best descriptions of the Art of Dying. In his Ecclesiastes Solomon tells his readers to 'Remember God' at all times and circumstances:

Remember your Creator
    in the days of your youth,
before the days of trouble come
    and the years approach when you will say,
    'I find no pleasure in them'—
before the sun and the light
    and the moon and the stars grow dark,
    and the clouds return after the rain;
when the keepers of the house tremble,
    and the strong men stoop,
when the grinders cease because they are few,

and those looking through the windows
   grow dim;
when the doors to the street are closed
   and the sound of grinding fades;
when men rise up at the sound of birds,
   but all their songs are faint;
when men are afraid of heights
   and of dangers in the streets;
when the almond tree blossoms
   and the grasshopper drags himself along,
   and desire no longer is stirred.
Then man goes to his eternal home
   and mourners go about the streets.

Remember him—before the silver cord is
   severed,
   or the golden bowl is broken;
before the pitcher is shattered at the spring,
   or the wheel broken at the well,
and the dust returns to the ground it came
   from,
   and the spirit returns to God who gave it.

Remember *Him*. Remember *your Creator* at all times.

The God of Abraham and Isaac is still the same God today, with the same demands upon all who claim to be His children. He is still 'the Fear of Isaac', who requires that all who choose to follow His purposes in the person of His Son, Jesus Christ, must put Him before parents and family at all times. When someone who wished to be a follower of Jesus said to Him: 'Lord, first let me go and bury my father'; Jesus replied: 'Let the dead bury their own dead, but you go and proclaim the kingdom of God.'

Dr Carl Jung, the noted psychologist, was an avid believer in *The Tibetan Book of the Dead*, and wrote a lengthy Introduction to it, in which he said it was his 'constant companion' for many years and the source of many of his ideas and insights. His description of the profoundly esoteric work is one of the best known and includes the following:

> The real purpose of this singular book is the attempt, which must seem strange to the educated European of the twentieth century, to enlighten the dead on their journey through the regions of the *Bardo* (purgatory). The Catholic Church is the only place in the world of the white man where any provision is made for the souls of the departed. Inside the Protestant camp, with its world-affirming optimism, we only find a few 'mediumistic circles', whose main concern is to make the dead aware of the fact that they *are* dead. But generally speaking, we have nothing in the West that is in any way comparable to the *Bardo Thodol* . . . As such, it forms a special chapter in the magical 'cure of the soul' which extends even beyond death . . .

The Judaeo-Christian Scriptures—despite what the Catholic Church teaches regarding influencing the souls of the departed in purgatory—assert unequivocally that at death the spirit returns to God who gave it. Solomon stated this several times in the Old Testament: 'No one has power over the spirit to retain the spirit, and no one has power in the day of death' (Eccles. 8:8 NKJV); 'Then the dust will return to the earth as it was, and the spirit will return to God who gave it' (Eccles. 12:7 NKJV).

The Art of Dying, therefore. is restricted to the time of living and does not extend into an intermediate state after death. When the curtain falls on the actor, so far as he or she is concerned the play of earthly life is ended, the audience leaves, and the lights are turned out. In life, the Apostle Paul said of all believers, 'We have been made a spectacle ('a theatre, or drama') to the whole universe, to angels as well as to men' (1 Cor. 4:9). Only those who have used their lives to prepare for a new play on a different stage of eternal life will share in its paradisal pleasures.

It was the Apostle Paul who was most explicit in dealing with the subject of dying and after-death experience. Regarding the moment of death, and what happens immediately afterwards, he wrote:

> Now we know that if the earthly tent we live in is destroyed, we have a building from God, an eternal house in heaven, not built by human hands. Meanwhile, we groan, longing to be clothed with our heavenly dwelling, because when we are clothed we will not be found naked . . .

In his *Commentary on the Second Epistle to the Corinthians*, Dr Handley Moule, the brilliant Fellow of Trinity, classical scholar and Lord Bishop of Durham, said of this Scripture (chapter 5):

> At death the spirit leaves the mortal body. The conscious self is 'absent from the body' or 'leaves its home in the body'. Between death and resurrection *that* connection is broken. But we are not to assume for certain that the outgoer is therefore formless, bodiless. It may be that the passage we have covered teaches us that an 'envelope' will be provided at once for the faithful soul, and we incline to think that it does. In that case the body of the resurrection will be, so to speak, the efflorescence of that envelope and continuous with it and with the present body, by the identity of the wearer, the subject. We dare not pronounce with certainty. But the angels have power to 'materialise' a bodily vehicle. So, the human spirit, yonder,

may well have a similar privilege, the
possession of an organ for its life and action,
pending the resurrection glory.

The Art of Dying, therefore, terminates with the
departure of the spirit. But just as categorically as the
Scriptures state that there is no earthly influence on the
departed spirit, they assert that the grave is not the end for
the body committed to it. Hilaire Belloc wrote:

> Because my faltering feet may fail to dare
> The first descendant of the steps of Hell
> Give me the Word in time that triumphs
>   there.
> I too must pass into the misty hollow
> Where all our living laughter stops; and hark!
> The tiny stuffless voices of the dark
> Have called me, till I needs must follow;
> Give me the Word and I'll attempt it well.

Give me the Word in time and I'll attempt it well! The
transcending Word that renews the mind here on earth, and
enables this mouldering body heading for dust to be
transformed into a glorified body on the other side of death.
The Paradise Factor.

CHAPTER 9

After Death

*T*he after-death state of immortality of the soul may be shown to have a relation to the living spiritual new-birth experience, similar to that which the new birth itself has to men and women in their 'natural' non-spiritual state.

But, first, it should be made clear that 'conversion' is not the same as 'regeneration', or new birth. Conversion is a change of direction only: in conversion the individual who is moving away from God 'turns back' to face God; while regeneration, or new birth, is a change of *quality*—from natural to spiritual, from immoral to moral, from the sinful womb of Satan-governed gestation to being born into a new life governed by Christ. In other words, a person may be 'converted' without being 'born again'. To be 'born again' means being born into the family of God through a new life in Christ.

'For to me, to live is Christ,' said Paul to the Philippians, 'and to die is gain.' Or, put another way: 'For me, to live on earth is Christ in me, and to die is *more Christ* with me.' He went on to add: 'I am torn between the two (that is, living or dying); I desire to die and be with Christ, which is better by far, but it is more necessary for you that I remain in the body.'

Conversion, then, is a change of direction and loyalty: from Satan to Christ. To many this means not much more than attending church regularly, and observing the better known teachings of Christ. But regeneration, or new life, is an implantation of the resurrected Christ in the individual which transforms him or her into being 'a new creation in Christ Jesus'. This is a very important distinction because after death it determines the transformation of the individual with 'Christ in' him or her into a 'glorified body' fit for Paradise and the presence of God.

This transformation after death into a 'glorified body', different from the physical shell, or 'tent', or 'envelope', used in one's lifetime, is explained by the Apostle Paul in a magnificent illustration in his first letter to the Corinthians:

> But someone will say, 'How are the dead raised up? And with what body do they come?' Foolish one, what you sow is not made alive unless it dies. And what you sow, you do not sow that body that shall be, but mere grain—perhaps wheat or some other grain. But God gives it a body as He pleases, and to each seed its own body (15:35–38 NKJV).

In other words, the grain or seed that is sown—small, hard, shrivelled, ugly—bears no relation to the glowing stalk of ripened wheat, or beauty of the full-blown rose. Yet the one is contained within the other, and is not only identified with it but is actually energised by it and a vital part of it. In our view, what Paul is saying is that the human body contains a vital element, analogous to the vital germ in a seed of corn, which does not perish when the enveloping husk of the seed dies in the soil, but which becomes the fruitful seed of the new shoot being transformed to live a new life in a new environment.

The Scottish preacher, P. T. Forsyth, declared in his book, *This Life and the Next*:

> The trouble about the doctrine of immortality has been increased by the fact that so many have turned it from an imperative task to a leisurely theme. It has passed from a practical task to be but a theoretical problem, from a Gospel to our will to be a riddle to our wits.

> From a 'concern' it has become an enigma.
> From a vocation it has turned a question. From
> a matter of conscience and duty it has become a
> matter of poetry and speculation. It has been
> made to rest not on the free grace of God but
> on the dim presumptions of man. The faith of it
> has turned from a gift of God to a result of ours.

Nietzsche declared that Paul had turned the gospel into
'the most despicable of all the most unfulfillable promises, the
most immodest doctrine of personal immortality'. Like so
many of Nietzsche's statements about the Scriptures it simply
betrays his ignorance of them, as well as of their God. It was
Jesus, before Paul, who emphasised resurrection, personal
immortality and retainable identity after death. Paul, as a
Hebrew scholar, only expanded on the theme. C. S. Lewis
has pointed out in *The Case for Christianity* that the Jews had
a long history of belief in immortality:

> From the earliest times the Jews, like many
> other nations, had believed that man possessed
> a 'soul' or *nephesh* separable from the body,
> which went at death to the shadowy world
> called Sheol . . . a land half unreal and
> melancholy like the Hades of the Greeks or the
> Niflheim of the Norsemen. From it shades
> could return and appear to the living, as
> Samuel's shade had done at the command of
> the Witch of Endor . . .

To the Jews, the kingdom of God was divided into two
ages: the present evil age in which they lived, and the one to
come when the Messiah would rule in peace and righteousness over all. To Jesus, the kingdom of God had arrived with
Him out of eternity, it was entirely the gift and work of God,
and its initiation with His incarnation was something new.
But, said Jesus, while it was a gift from God it was necessary

for individuals to *seek* this kingdom, to *strive* to enter, to *sacrifice* everything in order to enter it. In addition, every aspirant to the kingdom of God had to observe two conditions: one, they had to have a childlike spirit; and, two, they had to have a forgiving spirit. Finally, the kingdom of God was a condition of things on earth in which God's will was done as it was in heaven. It was heaven on earth; nothing less.

But even constant, daily association with Jesus as He did His miraculous works did not help His followers at the time to overcome their vicious fears with the virtuous fear of God.

When they saw Jesus walking on the water, the Scriptures record, 'They were *terrified*. "It's a ghost", they said, and cried out in *fear.*' (our italics here and following)

When they saw Jesus talk with Moses and Elijah on the Mount of Transfiguration 'they fell to the ground, *terrified*'.

When Jesus told them of His imminent death, and its significance, they were afraid: 'The Son of Man is going to be betrayed into the hands of men. They will kill him, but after three days he will rise.' Instead of bombarding Him with excited questions of 'How?' the Scriptures state: 'But they did not understand what he meant, *and were afraid to ask him about it.*'

Jesus' parting words to them at the Last Supper were that they were never to be afraid: 'Peace I leave with you; my peace I give you. I do not give to you as the world gives. Do not let your hearts be troubled and do not be afraid.'

But they would forget the words and the promises. In their vicious fear they would all reject all that Jesus had taught them and leave Him alone to face His own dark night of the soul. Peter would betray Him with curses, because of his fear of a servant girl. The beloved John would flee, but be the only man to turn up at the place of crucifixion with the women. They would all return to the city in fear when Jesus was dead and buried.

Then the Scripture records: 'On the evening of that first day of the week, when the disciples were together, *with the doors locked for fear of the Jews*, Jesus came and stood among them and said, "Peace be with you." '

The disciples, however, were not only afraid of their fellow Jews, they were also afraid of the risen Jesus. He had appeared among them through a locked door. The Scriptures state:

> They were terrified and frightened and supposed they had seen a spirit. And he said to them, 'Why are you troubled? And why do doubts arise in your hearts? Behold my hands and my feet, that it is I myself. Handle me and see, for a spirit does not have flesh and bones as you see I have.'

Earlier Jesus had told them that, in heaven, 'they neither marry nor are given in marriage, nor can they die any more'. But, on yet another occasion, when He met with them to partake of His last Passover Feast, having given them the bread and wine He said to them: 'I will not drink of this fruit of the vine from now until that day when I drink it new with you in my Father's kingdom.' So, the resurrected body was capable of drinking wine, in addition to being handled and identified.

Obviously, the resurrected body, the glorified body of after-death, is not the same as the physical body, whatever extra powers it may have. Whether the body is buried or burned after death, it disappears and cannot be reconstituted. If buried, it decomposes, eventually it becomes one with the soil, is absorbed into plants and grass, is eaten by insects and animals, and is no more. But so is the husk of the seed of grain and flower. It is the vital germ which is passed on and which becomes grain and rose, according to its original identity.

C. S. Lewis has written in *Beyond Personality*:

> The records represent Christ as passing after

death (as no man had passed before) neither into a purely, that is, negatively, 'spiritual' mode of existence nor into a 'natural' life such as we know, but into a life which has its own, new Nature. It represents Him as withdrawing six weeks later, into some different mode of existence . . . This presumably means that He is about to create that whole new nature which will provide the environment or conditions for His glorified humanity and, in Him, for ours . . . We must, indeed, believe the risen body to be extremely different from the mortal body; but the existence, in that new state, of anything that could be described as 'body' at all, involves some sort of spatial relations and in the long run a whole new universe. That is the picture—not of unmaking, but of remaking . . .

As Christians, it has been said, 'we die once, but are born twice'. To quote P. T. Forsyth (*God the Holy Father*) again:

The New Testament connects the idea of immortality with that of resurrection. Its nature is given in Christ's. It is not the resurrection of the flesh but of a body—not of matter but of form. The idea of resurrection means much more than repristination (recovering) of the old life under happier circumstances . . . Christ came back to give effect to what He had done. He came back, His body (not His flesh), His person came back to be the Holy Spirit of all that He had done. That is the real value of the resurrection. It gives the next life a realism drawn from its moral reality common and continuous with this . . . We take with us the character we made. All discussion of what body we come in is beside the point; and we have no data. What happens to this physical body is indifferent to faith, and it is left to reverence . . . We do not see the prospect (of immortality) as a field for imaginative enjoyment, nor as a food for our mere comfort. If Christ is our life our future is not our own. Our ruling passion is not greed of life. We do not do just what we must do to keep death at bay. We begin living the eternal life here, with its endless selfless energy, vaster than we feel, and surer than we know . . . The other life is not the negation and arrest of this. Nor is it mere restitution . . . it is not happiness and it is not power, but it is perfection—which is the growth of God's image and glory as our destiny.

This is the vision which inspired the Apostle Paul, especially when he said:

There are celestial bodies and terrestrial bodies; but the glory of the celestial is one, and the glory of the terrestrial is another. There is one glory of the sun, another glory of the moon, and another glory of the stars; for one star differs from another star in glory. So also is the resurrection of the dead. The body is sown in corruption, it is raised in incorruption. It is sown in dishonour, it is raised in glory. It is sown in weakness; it is raised in power. It is sown a natural body, it is raised a spiritual body.

The word 'glory' in the Scriptures is usually associated with radiancy of light. The face of Moses, when he had been in the presence of God, is recorded, 'the skin of Moses' face shone'. Also, when Moses and Elijah appeared with Jesus on the Mount of Transfiguration, it is said, 'As he (Jesus) prayed, the appearance of his face was altered, and his robe became white and glistening . . . and they saw his glory and the two men who stood with him.' So Moses and Elijah shared the same after-death radiant glory with Jesus.

One of the most beautiful examples of transformation takes place when a butterfly is born. At first simply a worm, crawling on the earth, it is tied to the lower world of dirt and darkness. Then it seems to die, folded up in the narrow shell of the chrysalis. Finally, out of that restraining 'coffin' it struggles forth into the glorious winged splendour of the dipping, darting creature that delights all eyes. It is no wonder that the Greeks called the soul and the butterfly by the same name.

In his second letter to the Corinthians Paul declares ringingly: 'But we all, with unveiled face, beholding as in a mirror the glory of the Lord, are being transformed into the same image from glory to glory.' We die and are buried as lowly caterpillars, with limited vision doomed to dissolution through the soil of this world. But, through Christ and the grace of God, we are being transformed to put on bodies of glory and beauty to grace the presence of God.

The Psalmist wrote prophetically:

> Ask of me and I will make the nations your inheritance, the ends of the earth your possession. You will rule them with a rod of iron, you will dash them to pieces like pottery. Therefore, you kings, be wise; be warned, you rulers of the earth. Serve the Lord with fear, and rejoice with trembling.

This ruling, or shepherdising, of the nations our Lord shares with those accompanying Him, His 'companions'—the 'Church which is his Spiritual Body'. The time has now come for them 'to judge the world'. The time, also, for the elect of Israel to enter into their promised inheritance. When He was with His followers on earth Jesus said to them:

You are those who have stood by me in my
trials. And I confer on you a kingdom, just as
my Father conferred one on me, so that you
may eat and drink with me at my table in my
kingdom *and sit on Thrones, judging the Twelve
Tribes of Israel.* (our italics)

Again, in the Apostle John's vision of the seven churches
in the book of Revelation, the promise of Jesus to His faithful
followers of all ages is: 'To him who overcomes and does my
will to the end, I will give authority over the nations—'He
will rule them with a rod of iron; he will dash them to pieces
like pottery'—just as I have received authority from my
Father.'

So the twelve apostles will rule over the faithful remnant
of the twelve tribes of Israel; and the overcoming Christian
believers will rule over 'the nations'. In John's vision he saw
thrones, such as he had seen earlier in the Revelation, with
the twenty-four elders, and those that sat on them 'had been
given authority to judge', and were, 'priests of God and of
Christ, and reign with him'. It is clear that it is God's elect
who are made 'kings and priests' destined to 'reign on earth'.
They are described by Peter:

You are a chosen people, a royal priesthood, a
holy nation, a people belonging in God . . . like
living stones, [you] are being built into a
spiritual house to be a holy priesthood, offering
spiritual sacrifices acceptable to God through
Jesus Christ . . .

In this millennial period all God's chosen elite will reign
with Christ, according to the lessons learned by them in their
maturing process of faith while living on the earth earlier.
Daniel, in his vision, saw 'the judgement seat', and the
dominion of the Beast taken away, and then 'the kingdom

and dominion, and the greatness of the kingdom under the whole heaven . . . given to the people of the saints of the Most High'.

The angel explicitly stated to the Apostle John that 'authority was given' to those sitting on the thrones; or, in other words, they were constituted judges with discretionary powers to act as those with divine authority. It is their responsibility to put into effect the commands of their reigning Lord, with the same shepherdising 'rod-of-iron' discipline, in order to eliminate the chaos of the world inherited from the rule of the Antichrist. They have to supervise the new politics, the new economics, the new social systems, the new forms of worship, out of which the new earth will be reconstructed on the basis of the laws of God and the teachings of the Lord Jesus Christ.

This is the time spoken of by the Apostle Paul when he said to the Corinthian believers: 'Do you not know that the saints will judge the world? And if you are to judge the world, are you not competent to judge trivial cases? Do you not know that we will judge angels? How much more the things of this life!'

Note that there are three groups of believers associated in this work of creational redemption, or regeneration of the world, with their Lord: there are the twenty-four elders on thrones, including the overcoming saints of past and present; there are the souls of them that are beheaded for the testimony of Jesus, the souls seen 'under the altar'; and there are those who, after these souls, 'are killed as they were'. All of these overcomers—fitted to rule by their faith and endurance, by their suffering and sacrifice—now assist their Lord in the administration of His millennial kingdom.

During this immortal administration, government-by-lie, duplicity, expediency and oppression will be swept away; and new, just, righteous laws based on love and truth introduced with firm discipline. Not only are there new government structures, based on the true value of men and women and their related responsibilities as laid down by God and as taught by Jesus, but also new policies regarding the animate and inanimate creation will be practised, thereby releasing enormous energies and wealth on an unprecedented scale—such as God promised to the Israelites under the Old Covenant, which they forfeited by their disobedience, but some of which was demonstrated to and by David and Solomon during their reigns. With the minds of men and women freed from the pressures of Satanic temptations and deceits there will be an upsurge and expansion of unimaginable creativity and innovation. Paradise regained.

This divine revolution also includes the possibility of never dying; of having glorified, incorruptible, corporeal bodies after the manner of our Lord, with heavenly qualities capable of sublimer joys. Jesus said while on earth:

> The people of this age marry and are given in marriage. But those who are considered worthy of taking part in that age, and in the resurrection from the dead, will neither marry nor be given in marriage, *and they can no longer die*, for they are like the angels. They are God's children, since they are children of the resurrection. (our italics)

There is a different criterion of sainthood during the millennium from that which is anticipated by many believers now. These latter look forward to singing psalms and hymns, and playing musical instruments, in some kind of endless heavenly church performance. But Jesus speaks of ruling, judging, administering, caring, working, in all aspects of making the earth a worthy place for the Lamb their King. As the Psalmist says:

> Therefore, you kings, be wise,
> be warned, you nations of the earth.
> Serve the Lord with fear
> and rejoice with trembling.

Kiss the Son, lest he be angry
and you be destroyed in your way,
for his wrath can flare up in a moment.
Blessed are all those who take refuge in him.

Or, as the prophet Isaiah says:

In that day the deaf will hear the words of the
      scroll,
and out of the gloom and darkness
the eyes of the blind will see.
Once more the humble will rejoice in the
      Lord,
the needy will rejoice in the Holy One of
      Israel.
The ruthless will vanish,
the mockers will disappear,
and all who have an eye for evil will be put
      down—
those who with a word make a man out to be
      guilty,
who ensnare the defender in court and
with false testimony deprive the innocent of
      justice . . .

There was also revealed to John in his vision in
Revelation how, at the end of this millennium of blessedness
and caring discipline, 'Satan will be released from his prison
and will go out to deceive the nations in the four corners of
the earth', in order to gather them once again into a battle
against God.

It seems incredible that men and women having
experienced all the paradisal delights of love and joy and
prosperity in a peaceful creation will yet again allow
themselves to be tempted and deceived—just as Adam and
Eve, with all the delights of the Garden of Eden, wanted the
one thing, knowledge of evil, that was forbidden them. They

do not want to know just the 'good' but also to know the 'evil' in the world.

Satan is set at liberty by God to demonstrate to men and women that, despite all the blessings of a sinless administration, there is still sufficient sin lurking in their hearts for them to choose it above the good provided freely by the Son of God. Like Satan himself, they do not want to serve in such an administration, but have ambitions to rule in an environment of their own choosing. In the freedom of the Messianic kingdom they choose to be in bondage to the wiles of Satan. It will be the final conclusive demonstration that men and women are not changed by the environment in which they live, but are creatures persuaded by individual selfishness and ambitions into rebellion against God.

Then follows the most solemn scene in the history of the world, when the eternal destinies of men and women are decided.

> Then I saw a great white throne and him who was seated on it. Earth and sky fled from his presence, and there was no place for them. And I saw the dead, great and small, standing before the throne, and books were opened. Another book was opened, which is the book of life. The dead were judged according to what they had done as recorded in the books. The sea gave up the dead that were in it, and death and Hades gave up the dead that were in them, and each person was judged according to what he had done. Then death and Hades were thrown into the lake of fire. The lake of fire is the second death. If anyone's name was not found written in the book of life, he was thrown into the lake of fire.

Unlike the first throne in John's earlier vision this one had no lesser thrones and other judges around, no seven spirits, no glass sea, no songs of joy. This throne had the same awesome majesty as the former, but was conspicuous for its whiteness only—symbolic of its unsullied justice. The Occupant on the throne is the same—One with no name, no form, but an eternal and indescribable Presence.

He was *there*, the focus of all minds and eyes, and everything in this earth and the heavens fled away at the almightiness of His Presence. There were no living creatures, no heavenly princes, no archangels. There is only the eternal Presence of God—and 'the rest of the dead' who did not take part in the first resurrection.

Those of the first resurrection have received their judgements and rewards, 'the second death has no power over them'; these of the second resurrection now await their judgements and punishments in undisguised terror. All the multitudes who ever sinned and never repented are released from their graves and spirit-prison to stand before the Almighty Judge to give an account of their individual actions as creatures to their Great Creator. Their works—perhaps unnoticed, or unrecorded, or expunged, while they lived—are now revealed with the opening of the books, but what is clear is that *their names are not in the book of life*.

The dead 'small or great' are there to be judged. Whether their sins were minor in their insignificant lives, or whether they were as great and public as Nero's or Hitler's, they are now revealed for divine judgement and eternal destiny.

Their sentences are followed by immediate execution—'thrown into the lake of fire'. It is idle to speculate whether this is physical or spiritual fire, and whether brimstone is the same as applied to fuel. Spiritual fire is the Almighty justice which burns eternally all dross and imperfections, all practised infractions and rebellions and evil of every kind against God's stated laws, in a restricted place peopled with created beings tormented by lost opportunities—'if only I had'. In this place, condemned to suffer the same penalty—but on a greater scale, because of their greater sin—are the great Beast and Beast-Prophet. To them are added death and

Hades, not in their impersonal capacity as elements of judgement, but as representative spirit-rulers who were the guardians of these places under the command of Satan.

With the final judgement ended, the Lord God Almighty gives a last command—at which the old heaven and earth burst into flames, and disappear in a last holocaust. Peter has described this:

> By the same word [of God] the present heavens and earth are reserved for fire, being kept for the day of judgement and destruction of ungodly men . . . But the day of the Lord will come like a thief. The heavens will disappear with a roar; the elements will be destroyed by fire, and the earth and everything in it will be laid bare.

This is the end of the old world. This is when the final and eternal Paradise begins.

It is important to note here, regarding the passing away of the old world, that nowhere do the Scriptures speak of it as termination of existence, but always of disappearance like dross in the purging or refining of gold. They all use the word for 'to pass'—as of a ship 'passing' through the sea, or 'passing' from one condition or place to another. It is never used in the sense of annihilation, or out of being; only of transition.

A careful reading of Peter's epistle shows that he also acknowledged this when he wrote of an earlier judgement of the world: 'The world that then was being overflowed with water, *perished* . . .' It is well known that the physical world at that time was not 'extinguished'; it was the *people* who perished, while the world itself continued.

And so John saw, after the final judgement, 'a new heaven and a new earth', the glorious regeneration of the redeemed world purposed by God from the beginning—a sinless, untainted Paradise. There is no sea in this New World, showing that there are to be no divisions between peoples and nations, no threatening uncertainties of communications.

In this New World John saw the Holy City, the New Jerusalem, coming down out of heaven from God, 'prepared as a bride beautifully dressed for her husband'. And he heard a voice from the throne saying:

> Now the dwelling of God is with men, and he will live with them. They will be his people, and God himself will be with them and be their God. He will wipe away every tear from their eyes. There will be no more death or mourning or crying or pain, for the old order of things has passed away.

We understand this to mean that the New Jerusalem is not fixed on earth, somehow replacing the geographical Jerusalem; but it is located *above* the earthly Jerusalem—like a 'marriage canopy', as Isaiah described it:

> Then the Lord will create over all of Mount Zion, and over those who assemble there, a cloud of smoke by day and a glow of glowing fire by night; *over all the glory will be a canopy* . . . (our italics)

The New Jerusalem will be as real a spiritual city as the Old Jerusalem is a physical city. It is 'the Holy City' in reality, and not just descriptively. It has specific dimensions. It has foundations, and walls, and streets, and inhabitants. It is the city that Abraham looked for 'which has foundations, whose maker and builder is God'. It is the city that all the saints have looked for when it is said: 'God prepared for them a city.' It is the city regarding which the writer to the Hebrews said, 'You are come to the city of the living God, the heavenly Jerusalem.' It is the place to which our Lord went to prepare for his own, when he promised them 'many dwelling-places'.

And this 'City' is at one and the same time the 'Bride, the Lamb's Wife'. A city is not only foundations and walls, streets and buildings; it is also the people who inhabit it. Those who reign with our Lord—the Patriarchs, the Apostles, the Overcoming Church, the Remnants—move between the New Jerusalem and the Old Jerusalem, and throughout the nations, according to their responsibilities and administrative tasks. As Isaiah saw in his vision:

> Behold, I will create
> a new heaven and a new earth.
> The former things will not be remembered,
> nor will they come to mind.
> But be glad and rejoice for ever
> in what I will create,
> for I will create Jerusalem to be a delight
> and its people a joy.
> I will rejoice over Jerusalem
> and take delight in my people;
> the sound of weeping and dying
> will be heard in it no more.

Paradise!

EPILOGUE

Spiritual Revolution Essential

*I*t will be obvious from the theme and emphases of this book that, if Paradise is ever to be attained in the nation's experience, a revolution will have to take place in society. It is equally obvious from the Report of the Council of Europe's recommendations regarding dealing with the addiction problem that these, too, require some form of social and political revolution before they could be implemented (see Appendix). Probably that is why they have been ignored.

While all that we have written about here is possible of attainment for the simplest and lowliest member of society, as Jesus affirmed, yet we realise it cannot be obtained without a transformation of the individual and, by extension, the family, community or nation of which he or she is a part. That was true of Jesus' message in His time; it was true of His followers immediately afterwards as they launched the gospel of Christ. It has been true historically whenever there has been a return to fundamental Scriptural truths.

Søren Kierkegaard said that there are two types of revolution: the really passionate revolution, which tears everything down; and the other bloodless kind, which leaves everything standing 'but cunningly emptied of significance'. It is the latter which has afflicted the West in the past century; the negative revolution which occurs in any nation when it loses its vision and values through a combination of complacency, hubris, neglect and cynicism. Dostoevski described it in his *Diary of a Writer*:

An ethical idea has always preceded the birth
of a nation . . . and when, with the passage of
time, a nation's spiritual ideal is sapped, that
nation falls with all its civil statutes and ideals.

That is what has happened to Britain and the United
States in our lifetime.

But there is a third type of revolution, a spiritual
revolution—the turning from material-oriented to the
spiritual-directed, from deliberate self-will to conscious God-
will—which has been described by the Russian exile,
Alexandr Solzhenitsyn, in *From Under the Rubble*, as 'a moral
change . . . to inward development':

This turn toward *inward* development, the
triumph of inwardness over outwardness, if it
ever happens, will be a great turning point in
the history of mankind, comparable to the
transition from the Middle Ages to the
Renaissance. There will a complete change not
only in the direction of our interests and
activities but in the very nature of human
beings (a change from spiritual dispersal to
spiritual concentration), and a greater change
still in the character of human societies. If in
some places this is destined to be a
revolutionary process, these revolutions will
not be like the earlier ones—physical, bloody
and never beneficial—but will be moral
revolutions requiring both courage and
sacrifice, though not cruelty—a new
phenomenon in human history, of which little
is yet known and which as yet no one has
prophetically described in clear and precise
forms . . .

In 1961, in New York, 74 nations signed the Single

National Convention on Narcotic Drugs. In 1970 the 19-nation Council of Europe (Strasbourg) concluded: '. . . in all countries there has been an upsurge in the number of drug dependents which has now attained the dimensions of an epidemic', and went on to state:

> It is important to have in mind that this subject includes not only psychological and medical but also social, educational, cultural and political aspects. The increase in the dimensions of the problem can be looked upon as a symptom that there is something very wrong with society.
> *The problem is a problem neither of youth nor one of drugs, but a problem of a whole society and an entire lifestyle shared by young and old alike.*
> (our italics)

The unconscious irony of the 19-nation Council of Europe's Report quoted above is that, in delineating and defining the problem, and concluding that it is Western society itself that is 'sick', they ignore or neglect in their conclusions to mention the very element which could cure that sickness: the spiritual factor.

Note that they say, 'It is important to have in mind that this subject [the drug abuse problem] includes not only psychological and medical but also social, educational, cultural and political aspects'—no mention of 'spiritual'. Yet the specialist professionals included in their list—psychologists, psychiatrists, sociologists, educationalists, writers and politicians—all have had exclusive access, finance and opportunities to solve the drug problem for the past thirty years of its rising menace, with lamentable failure as the result. If that is not blind analytical stupidity and anti-spiritual prejudice, we don't know what is.

It could also be said that ecclesiastics of almost every persuasion have been represented on all the bodies included in the professions listed in the Report quoted above; and that, therefore, through their presence, the 'spiritual' was considered and is part of the failure. But the very fact of the exclusion from mention of ecclesiastics in the Report is indicative of the contempt for their inadequate and stereotypical secularised Judaeo-Christian contribution in the minds of their peers.

Where religious organisations have set up rehabilitation centres these have usually followed the orthodox formulae postulated by their unsuccessful secular counterparts. The statistics of success of Christian rehabilitation organisations are little better—and sometimes worse—than those of non-Christian agencies. The chief reason for this lies in their slavish conformity to the secular Freudian, Jungian, Behaviourist, or empirical, psychotherapies, with only an added superficial dash of neo-Christian practice, depending on the dogmatic orientation of the organisation.

In a comparative statistical study of the treatment of heroin addiction by the leading Christian treatment organisation, Teen Challenge, and the regime of Transactional Analysis, seventeen subjects were assigned at random to each of three treatment regimes—No Treatment (NT), Teen Challenge (TC), and Transactional Analysis (TA); with the subject in the last two groups being under treatment for six to twelve months. The purpose of the experiment was to determine whether these approaches had a differential effect on heroin addiction. A score on a standardised questionnaire and recidivism rates, measured over a 29-month period, were used as an index of the effectiveness of each treatment. The data, as measured by the treatment given, the questionnaire results and recidivism rates, gave unequivocal support for three findings:

1. that TC is an *effective* programme of treatment;
2. that TA is a *very effective* method of treatment;

3. that, based on the lower questionnaire score when compared to NT and the lower recidivism rates, TA is the best regime of treatment for heroin addiction of the three treatments investigated. (our italics)

Recidivism rates, computed from the TC and TA records over a 29-month period and being defined as again returning to drugs, were for TC and TA programmes 32 per cent and 16 per cent respectively. The author's conclusion is well worth noting by all Christians working in the drug field:

While it is true that the TC programme seems to help the addict increase his self-awareness, it is also true that the approach deals with heroin and other addictions in a repressive manner, i.e. the motivation of the addict has been changed because of his conversion to Christ whom he accepts as his Lord and Master and accordingly views drug-taking as a sin. It appears that dealing with drug addiction in this manner masks the symptoms and aetiology, and in doing so does not get at the real causes which led up to the addict becoming addicted to heroin and other drugs. Thus, the addict's belief in Christ, even though sincere and real, becomes a drug substitution which often never grows beyond that little spark of embryonic faith . . .

Addicts have often had a rather poor relationship with their earthly father. These negative feelings which come about as the result of the poor interpersonal relationship between father and addict could very well be carried over to the matter of their faith in Christ. Thus loss of faith would occur because the addict had only had a change of

environment, conversion, undergone detoxification, and was now beginning to feel better
because of regular hours, and eating habits. But
the root causes which had allowed that
individual addict to become addicted in the
first place had not been acted upon in
psychotherapy . . .[1]

Yet it should be noted that, having paid careful attention
to such reports and dangers, it is the 'spiritual' solutions
already being practised which are giving the most successful
results in every country. Most of the existing programmes in
any Freudian, Jungian, Behaviourist or empirical unit treating
addictions show ten per cent success after ten years—if
'success' is judged by freedom from all drug addictions,
including methadone. But the 'spiritually-based' Alcoholics
Anonymous—founded by an Oxford Group Christian—and
its sister organisation Narcotics Anonymous, are statistically
far more successful. Narcotics Anonymous is not a religious
organisation, yet in its introduction to the official manual it is
stated:

Based on our experience, we believe that every
addict, including the 'potential' addict, suffers
from an incurable disease of body, mind and
spirit. We were in the grip of a hopeless
dilemma, *the solution of which is spiritual in
nature*. Therefore, this book will deal with
spiritual matters . . . (our italics)

Fundamental to both of these treatment programmes is
the centrality of God, and confession of personal
powerlessness otherwise to deal with addictions, as follows:

---

1. 'Heroin Addiction: Teen Challenge vs Transactional Analysis: A Statistical Study',
US Journal of American Scientific Affiliation, Vol. 25, No. 3, 1973.

We came to believe that a Power greater than ourselves could restore us . . .

We made a decision to turn our will and lives over to the care of God . . .

We admitted to God, to ourselves, and to another human being the exact nature of our wrongs . . .

We were entirely ready to have God remove all these defects of characters . . .

We humbly asked Him to remove our shortcomings . . .

We sought through prayer and meditation to improve our conscious contact with God as we understood Him, praying only for a knowledge of His will for us and power to carry that out . . .

But the God that most of those who enter the AA or NA programmes pray to is an unknown God, a 'Power greater than ourselves', a 'God as we understand Him'. At the meetings there is little or no attempt made to identify that God; only to fish in the sea of divine immanence hoping for some form of lucky spiritual 'catch'. It is a far cry from being 'kissed by God', from discovering the 'Paradise Factor'.

The churches as they are presently organised are not equipped to deal with the seriousness of the national drug problem. What have they to offer the addicted? A sermon on Sunday? A mention in prayer? An occasional visit from pastor or priest? A referral to Alcoholics Anonymous or Narcotics Anonymous?

The most recent study of the National Institute on Drug Abuse in the United States, in three programmes in New York, Philadelphia and Baltimore, was reported in the *New York Times* (7 September, 1988):

. . . Of 388 patients who remained in treatment for one year or more, 71 per cent had stopped intravenous drug use. Of those who left the methadone programmes, 82 per cent quickly returned to intravenous drug use.

But the success of the programmes varied widely, depending on how well they were operated, the report found. 'The success of the programmes depends on the experience of the director, the morale of the staff, and the support they are getting from the government', said Dr John C. Ball, who headed the project at the Institute's Addiction Research Centre in Baltimore. 'In some areas we have states and cities that are not very supportive at all.'

The newspaper article went on to report 'formidable obstacles', such as the reluctance of local and state politicians to fight community opposition to building treatment clinics in their neighbourhoods, budget cuts, lack of personnel, mismanagement of current treatment programmes, and concluded:

. . . The most daunting drug treatment task of all is addiction to crack. The authorities have linked crack addiction to crime, and AIDS experts have blamed them for contributing to the spread of the disease.

Methadone cannot be used to treat cocaine or crack addiction. Such patients are treated in programmes that do not use a substitute drug, relying on individual psychotherapy, group therapy and residential care of from 28 days to 18 months.

Four years ago 'crack' was a drug problem restricted to only two or three large American cities—Los Angeles, New York, Washington. Now it is a nationwide epidemic reaching into the country's rural areas, with no treatment process available.

'Crack' is a mixture of cocaine, baking soda and pharmaceutical 'stretchers', combined to produce a nugget of intensified euphoria. It has been called 'the fast food version of cocaine', sells for about five dollars a shot, and gives an intense 'high', rapid addiction, and an accelerated descent into drug-induced dissolution.

It is immensely popular, and is now being marketed by young teenagers as dealers, who can make an easy thousand dollars a day in profits—often encouraged by their parents. These young dealers stand on the streets, visit school playgrounds, cruise in cars, deliver orders to offices. The police cannot cope with them. They carry paging bleepers with them, and the linking paging bleepers are now being carried by youthful associates in school classrooms, who seek the orders inside the schools and have them delivered to the school gates.

Some parents in Washington were so incensed by the open drug-dealing, and the associated violence and crime in their areas, that they contacted a Muslim religious organisation, the 'Nation of Muslim' for help. Ironically, one of the two city districts to do so was known as 'Paradise Manor'! The Muslims quickly and effectively got rid of the drug dealers with a mixture of rough-handling and street patrols. They have since joined with the police in an unusual alliance to drive out the drug dealers and gunmen who terrorised the one thousand houses in the area.

'Lift up your eyes,' Jesus admonished His followers, 'and see the fields ready to harvest.' Self-centred communities with lack of compassion—although the same communities will have families with substance abuse problems, and certainly will be attending a variety of local churches; self-centred local and state politicians reluctant to take action lest they lose the self-centred community votes; lack of skilled and caring personnel, and mismanagement by existing project leaders; overworked, or cynical, or corrupt police who are understaffed, underpaid and unequipped to deal with the complexities of the drug network—here is a mission field of monumentally important proportions, and it is one that can be attacked by both enthusiastic youth and retired elderly of all classes.

Both in the United States, and in the United Kingdom, the most effective measures have been taken by parents disillusioned by officials and doctors, and determined to do something about the drug problem themselves. The current religiously-orientated voluntary treatment agencies are usually based on outdated and inadequate psycho-therapeutic theories, and are not aware of the important medical and scientific advances of the past twenty years which have made standard treatment and rehabilitation practices obsolete.

It is now possible to detoxify from all chemical addictions, *without supplementary addictive drugs*, within a period of ten days or less instead of weeks or months; but there is no current follow-up rapid psychotherapeutic programme that is successful. One well-known US West Coast chain of treatment clinics admits a *100 per cent relapse rate* after completion of their treatment regime. The field is wide open for experienced, enthusiastic and informed Christians with vision and conviction and commitment applying the principles outlined in this book.

One of Britain's leading experts on the drug problem, Bing Spear—for eight years Chief Inspector of the government's Home Office Drugs Branch—has given his opinion regarding the drug problem in Britain. In a newspaper report (*Independent*, 9 May, 1988) he declared:

> After years of political neglect, the politicians
> in the early eighties responded to proper public
> concern and not to the drug problem itself. We
> have to accept that we have failed. And we
> have to ask why. It is no longer any good to
> rely on enforcement to solve the problem.

There is a limit to what enforcement can do
and that limit has now been realised. We
should start to look at it as a broad social issue.

But in our opinion it is not enough to look at it only as 'a
broad social issue'—that has been researched into the ground
by a variety of committees set up for the purpose in different
countries—unless it is taken to include the *spiritual* aspects as
well. The Western nations are now facing a political and
social crisis due to a problem rooted in the spiritual, as has
been shown; and until that issue of resolving the demand for
drugs has been addressed the situation must continue to get
worse.

One of the leading Colombian drug barons, Carlos
Lehder Rivas, has stated that 'drugs are now the Third
World's atomic bomb', and boasted: 'Coca has been
transformed into a revolutionary weapon for the struggle
against American imperialism. The Achilles' heel of
imperialism is the drugs of Colombia.'

When George and his television colleagues, Adrian
Cowell and Chris Menges, made a documentary, *The Opium
Trail*, on the subject of drug trafficking from the 'Golden
Triangle' of Burma, Thailand and Laos to Hong Kong in the
1960s, it was estimated that there were some 15,000 soldiers
moving about 700 tons of raw opium a year, to be processed
into morphine and heroin and selling for profits to the
Chinese criminal 'triads' of some US$2 billion in Hong Kong.

Twenty years later, in the London *Observer* (8 May,
1988), it was reported that the Shan private army General
Khun Sa, in charge of the drug trafficking from Burma, would
be producing 1200 *tons* of raw opium, to be refined into 120
tons of pure 'No. 4' heroin for the world market. In an
interview with the *Observer*'s correspondent, General Khun
Sa said:

People call me a drugs warlord. They do not
want to know that we are fighting a war of

independence against the brutal regime of Ne Win (the Burmese strongman). I am recruiting and training 400 soldiers every 16 weeks. When we are strong enough, we will give the Burmese an ultimatum to leave our country. Our strength, our political power, will have to come out of the barrel of a gun, as Mao Tsetung proclaimed.

Until fairly recently the drug trade was largely the province of vicious and avaricious criminals, mostly from the Sicilian and Corsican mafias in Europe, and the Chinese criminal secret society 'triads' in Asia, and the Latin American drug barons. But in the 1980s various terrorist organisations around the world began to recognise the political potential offered by the criminally organised drug trade, as drug addicts everywhere showed they were prepared to pay the price—socially, politically, financially—to obtain the necessary drug to satisfy their craving. A US Drug Enforcement Administration report noted that 'rural insurgents, urban terrorists, liberation movements, arms traffickers, subversives, left- and right-wing political groups and high-level officials acting on behalf of their governments' were now deeply involved in the drugs trade.

A survey in the US News and World Report (4 May, 1987) was even more ominous. It reported a world-wide link-up between drug traffickers and terrorists:

In the nether world of narco-terrorism there are three main protagonists: the insurgent groups such as the IRA, the Tamils and the Sikhs; the intelligence services and officials or governments bent on exporting revolution such as Cuba and Iran; and, finally, dope gangsters like Lehder of Colombia, who use political violence and classic terror tactics to further their aims. The three types of narco-terrorists invariably traffic in weapons, launder money, share intelligence, trade false passports, provide each other with safe havens, and render assistance in a loose global alliance.

Meanwhile, the countries which produce the drugs—sophisticated Western nations with pharmaceutical corporations producing 'designer' prescription preparations, as well as primitive Third World nations with illicit organisations distributing processed 'nature' drugs for gangsters—spiral downwards into political crisis and economic ruin. The desperate South American Colombian government placed a full-page advertisement in the *New York Times* during the 1989 US Presidential elections urging both candidates:

> The real question is—will you go beyond efforts to stop the supply before it crosses your borders and beat the narco-problem at its final destination, the US consumer?

> Without demand there is no supply. That is a simple law of economics . . . The plain truth is that we will never win this war without the support of every American. The menace will not go away until the demand goes away . . .

And the whole world has observed the United States' impotence over the notorious drug trafficking President of Panama and the Prime Minister of the Bahamas. Even although they have been restrained and punished the drugs have continued to pour into the United States and elsewhere in response to the demand.

Yet, governments are still reluctant to take any substantive action to deal with the drug problem until there is a public movement of protest. When public concern erupts in any city or region, especially when it begins to figure prominently in the media, there is a flurry of interest in government or opposition circles as political votes come under threat. Then specious statements are made to the media, false assurances are given to the parents in the cities or regions, a few cosmetic gestures are made in the fields of law enforcement and education, until the protest diminishes. Sometimes yet another government advisory body is set up—all participants taken from the same professional groups who have failed in the past, and usually dominated by the psychiatrists who are in charge of the unsuccessful drug units, and who are using addictive drugs as part of their supposed curative treatments.

Regarding one of the most widely used official methadone treatment programmes, a leading international authority, Dr Stanton Peele, has stated emphatically in *Love and Addiction*: 'Methadone maintenance is one example of this wrong-headed approach to combating addiction . . . Its founders, Drs Dole and Nyswander, note that methadone maintenance's impact has been minimal "at best" . . .'

The most effective contribution has been when the outraged parents of a country have set up local vigilante groups—despite protests from officials and police—to combat dealers operating in their neighbourhoods; and also self-help groups to study and produce their own monitored solutions. In Italy, the mothers in Padua set up their own movement called 'Mothers of Despair' to patrol the streets, defy the drug dealers, pressure the reluctant politicians, and shame the police into action, on behalf of their addicted children.

Other countries have churches where groups of concerned individuals have set up housing associations to buy up derelict 'crack' houses that were being used by gun-carrying drug dealers as distribution centres for the cocaine packets, and then renting the voluntarily remodelled houses to poor but honest people who will keep the street drug-free.

It will take the same kind of commitment from the public in Britain and the United States to get rid of the hated pusillanimous politicians, unscrupulous gangsters, cynical policemen and unprincipled media propagandists corrupting the systems in their countries to their own selfish advantage.

In the United States it was recently demonstrated that the government officials were in collusion with doctors to deliberately drug children (without their parents knowing about it in many instances) in order to keep them under control, rather than use spiritual methods. According to a report in the *Journal of the American Medical Association* (21 October, 1988), the Baltimore County Health Department and Johns Hopkins University recorded 6 per cent—or one in every seventeen children—were being treated by the addictive drug Ritalin. The findings suggested that almost a million elementary school children around the country were being treated by the stimulant, and the numbers were increasing. The researchers declared: 'Medication for hyperactive children in the United States has emerged from its minor treatment role in the 1960s *to become the dominant child mental-health intervention in the late 1980s.*' (our italics)

What the psychiatrists have done is create the condition known as 'attention-deficit hyperactivity syndrome' ('the syndrome interferes with the child's ability to pay attention in class and causes disruptive behaviour'), and prescribe Ritalin to control it. It was the psychiatrists who earlier had produced the self-indulgent theories which contributed towards the children becoming undisciplined and anti-social, and who, of course, benefited financially by prescribing the drugs on such a national scale to a new generation.

Reporting the survey, the *Philadelphia Inquirer* said:

> At least 13 lawsuits have been filed around the country on behalf of parents distressed by the effects of the drug on their children. The suits have charged that the drug numbed the children's senses, produced amnesia and the loss of appetite, and even led to psychotic behaviour . . . A Los Angeles-based group called the Citizen's Commission on Human

> Rights . . . has campaigned aggressively against
> the drug . . . given to 14 million children to
> keep them in 'chemical strait-jackets' . . .
> highly addictive, predisposing children to
> delinquency.

Will the President, or his department officials, take
official action against the psychiatrists? Will he limit any of
the other practices of the medical establishment which
induce and perpetuate the addictions? An article in the US
journal, the *New Republic*, about the same time declared:

> The health industry brought all the major illicit
> drugs into popular usage . . . Most of their
> narcotics prosecutions in this century targeted
> the notorious 'dope doctors' and their
> confederates in the medicinal trade . . .
>
> Quite apart from tobacco, alcohol and the
> illicit narcotics, health experts have made
> Americans a heavily drugged people even in
> proportion to wealth. In 1968 retailed
> pharmacists alone filled *1.56 billion*
> prescriptions for restricted drugs . . . next come
> 132 million 'psycho-therapeutics', a medical
> euphemism for uppers and downers;
> prescriptions for 112 anti-depressants, led by an
> expensive pick-me-up called Elavil, have risen
> fivefold in the past generation . . .

In a highly publicised situation in the city of Detroit in
the United States the local citizens got fed up with the lack
of concern of all supposedly responsible authorities and did
something about it. It was a quiet, working-class neighbourhood, where people grew azaleas and children skipped with
their ropes, until it was changed by bands of drug-dealing
teenagers carrying guns and selling drugs in broad daylight.
Two neighbours got tired of the drug dealing and 'turf wars'

and in desperation burned down the house of a notorious 'crack'-dealing gang after several attempts to get the police to do something had failed. The Prosecutor said he would not permit law-abiding citizens to break the law of the land on the 'theory that they were frustrated'. But the foreman of the jury trying the two men, who acquitted them, said the verdict was their way of telling city officials 'that more had to be done to fight drugs'.

The case stirred up considerable controversy across the country as large numbers of people under pressure elsewhere applauded what the two men had done. A call-in poll found that 87 per cent of the callers thought that the burning of the 'crack' house was justified. In other places in Detroit citizens armed themselves with baseball bats and metal pipes to attack dealers and drug-dealing houses. One professor of sociology stated: 'This kind of behaviour is a form of public communication. It is a bargaining chip for the citizens, who are saying to the authorities, "Unless you take action we will." '

The lawyer who represented one of the men said:

> What is occurring in the streets now is anarchy. Should you just let criminals prey on your kids and shoot guns in the middle of the day until the police get around to it? No one is going to buy that. It's a sad commentary on our society if people have to do this.

What is happening in the United States is also practised in the United Kingdom. The psychiatrists use the addictive drugs methadone and Valium and Ativan with medical establishment and government approval. At the same time they make little or no provision for desperate parents and families seeking help with their addiction problem. In fact, they go out of the way to put stumbling blocks in the way of anguished parents trying to do something. The police accuse them of 'the dangers of vigilantism' when anguished parents take matters into their own hands, while the police themselves are rarely available for protection, or able to provide any solution other than demanding more money for more policemen or customs officials.

This is what is happening to Western societies particularly, whose civilisation and culture was based on Judaeo-Christian values, and who have allowed these to be first eroded, and then destroyed. Books and broadcasts, magazines and films, casually denigrate almost every worthwhile biblical value.

In a centre-page article in *The Times* (February, 1990), under the headline, 'Moral Sabotage Parents Cannot Withstand', Ronald Butt declared:

> Until about 25 years ago, the standards of responsibility that most parents took for granted in the home were reinforced by those of the school, broadcasting, the media and, for the most part, entertainment.
>
> That is no longer so. Children are subjected to an ugly cultural climate which accepts, as facts of life to be tolerated, bad manners, violence in speech and deed, casual sex and the ethics of do-as-you-please. The minds of the young have been opened to moral brutality to an extent inconceivable a few decades ago, and children are affected not only directly but by the erosion of the values of adults generally . . .

For the past twenty or thirty years it has been an accepted practice—unchallenged by national political, media and church leaders—to disparage and discredit the desire to help one's neighbours by sneeringly calling it 'do-gooding'; forgetting or ignoring that it was said by a leading political authority: 'All it needs for the eventual triumph of evil is for good people to do nothing.' Ironically, there was an item on a recent television news programme, when the head of the Girl

Guide movement was being interviewed regarding the protested incorporation of girls into the Boy Scouts movement. She was strongly objecting to the decision, and in the course of her remarks said: 'Our girls have not been "goody-goodies" for some time now'!

Now that the 'do-badders' have their murderous knives at the throats of every family in the nation in the persons of the unscrupulous criminals, ubiquitous drug dealers, corrupt police and politicians and officials, avaricious doctors and platitudinous priests and pastors, these same thoughtlessly cursing and contemptuous individuals, who undermined the values of home and community and society by their own conversation and conduct at their local pubs or smart cocktail parties, are exposed as pathetically bewildered, inadequate and afraid—and blaming everybody else but themselves.

The present drugs crisis is the nation's despairing chemical cry for freedom from this self-wrought satanic prison of the mind, and for help to find the true spiritual revolutionary Paradise Factor. In his book, *Addiction: the Human Condition*, William Lentners writes:

> Freedom that is only freedom *from*, with no thought of freedom *for*, freedom that is compulsively sought rather than graciously received, is no freedom at all. It is a terrible burden under which those who bear it eventually stumble into the abyss of habituation . . . The paradox of freedom is critical to the understanding of the human addiction. Addiction can be seen as a search for freedom turned in on itself . . .

To be spiritually free from the bondage of chemical or behavioural addiction does not mean to be absolutely free from all restraints. When Jesus said: 'You shall know the truth and the truth shall make you free', He went on to add two conditions which made this freedom contingent: one, 'if you continue in my word'; and, two, 'if you are my disciples indeed'.

Jesus was not just declaring a principle of universal value, important as that might be; for example, that the observance of a recognised standard of veracity in personal, group, national, or international relationships would set individuals, communities and nations free from the bondage and consequences of lying, deceit, and the hypocrisies of their daily cynical practices. He was categorically asserting that it is possible for an individual to *know the truth* as a divine absolute which Jesus Himself had received from God, and to *do truth* in daily experience. As a result that individual would be delivered from all the consequences of experienced bondage.

Archbishop William Temple said in *Nature and Destiny*: 'The way to spiritual freedom . . . is always by surrender to the object—to the real facts in the life of science, to the goal or cause in practical conduct, to God as He reveals Himself in worship.'

'Set Free!' That does not mean just 'to cope with', or 'live with' fear and failure and weakness—'no-fault' or otherwise. It does not mean 'Just Say No' to a particular chemical. It means to live as Christ Himself lived—triumphantly; with a knowledge of divine acceptance and divine power to overcome all the many weaknesses as a demonstration of the indwelling power of an Almighty God.

A person has to have a belief system if he or she is to have values—a belief system that is more than a mere mental assent to a set of theological propositions. A value may be defined as: a belief freely chosen from among alternatives, after careful consideration of the consequences of each alternative; a belief that is prized, so that the person freely choosing is satisfied with the choice; a belief that is important enough so that the person will publicly affirm the choice; and a belief that is acted on repeatedly over a period of time, and incorporated into a person's behaviour.

As Plato noted over two thousand years ago, a

government that cannot look after the best interests of its citizens is a useless appendage. For two thousand years it has been the stated goal of nations that the state is 'a means to happiness'. The aim of the kingly art or science, said Plato, is 'to make men happy, mainly by making them good; for, if they are virtuous, they must surely be happy'. Aristotle said that the 'aim of politics is to make men happy':

> It ordains which of the sciences should be studied in a state, and which class of citizens should learn and up to which point they should learn them; and we see even the most highly esteemed of capacities to fall under this, for example, strategy, economics, rhetoric; now, since politics uses the rest of the sciences, and since again it legislates as to what we are to do and what we are to abstain from, the end of this science (the production of happiness) must include those of the others.

When the founding fathers of the American nation drafted their constitution they stated the goal in the Declaration of Independence: '. . . all men are endowed by their Creator with certain inalienable rights; that among these are life, liberty, *and the pursuit of happiness*. That to secure these rights, governments are instituted among men . . .'

But, significantly, eleven years later, when the Preamble to the Constitution was declared, it had deleted this goal: 'We, the people of the United States, in order to form a more perfect union, establish justice, insure domestic tranquillity, provide for the common defence, *promote general welfare* . . . do ordain and establish this Constitution of the United States of America . . .'

The goal of 'pursuit of happiness' was subtly changed to 'promote general welfare', and, with the change, the spiritual dimension as a national goal was lost. The 'welfare state' emphasises the physical needs of the people, and the political leaders can then jettison their responsibilities for the spiritual dimensions requisite in 'the pursuit of happiness' and leave them to religious leaders. The acquisition and practice of spiritual values is no longer a national aspiration of good statesmanship, but an unenforced ecclesiastical option.

This was forcibly impressed on us when we attended a high-level government meeting in London to discuss the drug problem with a group of the Government's 'official experts'. After an hour or so of the usual polite circumlocution, with a suggestion to Meg that she might join one or more of the official committees studying the problem, George pointed out the need for a positive change of addiction treatment practices, to include a spiritual dimension.

The chairman, with barely concealed contempt, said: 'But, Mr Patterson, you don't really expect *government* to fund your spiritual treatment, do you?'

George had a long experience of supercilious officials, and he retorted: 'I don't see why not. You have spent the past twenty years or more funding *unspiritual* and *unsuccessful* treatments, to my knowledge. If you give money to Freudians and Marxists, why not Christians? Isn't this supposed to be a Christian country?'

The three great political revolutions in the West in the past three centuries—France, Britain and America—arose out of *spiritual* concerns with human conditions; and were then allowed by default to be taken over by *secularists* who re-defined the aims and policies of the nations to suit their secularist 'political' convictions. It only needed another step to argue speciously that 'the constitutional separation of Church and State' meant keeping ecclesiastics from commenting on 'political matters', and politicians from interfering with 'ecclesiastical affairs'. The politicians were then left free to pursue whatever mendacity furthered their expedient interests.

In the Introduction to his book, *The Acquisitive Society*, Professor R. H. Tawney writes:

If the medicine of the constitution ought not to be made its daily food, neither can its daily food be made its medicine. There are times which are not ordinary, and in such times it is not enough to follow the road. It is necessary to know where it leads, and, if it leads to nowhere, to follow another. The search for another involves reflection, which is uncongenial to the bustling people who describe themselves as practical, because they take things as they are and leave them as they are. But the practical thing for a traveller who is uncertain of his path is not to proceed with the utmost rapidity in the wrong direction; it is to consider how to find the right one. And the practical thing for a nation which has stumbled upon one of the turning-points of history is not to behave as though nothing very important were involved, as if it did not matter whether it turned to the right or to the left, went up hill or down dale, provided that it continued doing with a little more energy what it has done hitherto; but to consider whether what it has done hitherto is wise, and, if it is not wise, to alter it . . . If it is to make a decision which will wear, it must travel beyond the philosophy momentarily in favour with the proprietors of its newspapers. Unless it is to move with the energetic futility of a squirrel in a revolving cage, it must have a clear apprehension both of the deficiency of what is, and of the character of what ought to be . . . It must, in short, have Principles.

The Apostle Paul was as aware of this human trend in the first century as we are today, because it was the subject of wide public comment and debate. But he did not devote his great intelligence to devising a neo-Christian Platonic or Aristotelian philosophy, or to forming a Judaeo-Christian reforming political party. He declared that, with the coming of Jesus Christ, and His death and resurrection, God had done a revolutionary 'new thing' in history—but in keeping with the ancient Scriptures; He had provided, in sending His Son, Jesus, the means and the power to alter all individuals and circumstances to conform to a divine ideal.

What it involved was a total change of direction for individuals and nations, from being self-centred to being God-centred, as Jesus Christ had demonstrated in His person and life and teachings. Because this was an extremely difficult thing to do, God had also provided the ability to do it. All it required from the individual was a willingness to accept God's freely offered gift of power. The Apostle John described it: 'As many as received him (into their lives) *to them gave he power to become the sons of God*, even to them that believe on his name.' (our italics)

When contemporary governments in the West fail to do something about the recommendations of some of the advisory committees they have already accumulated, other than just appointing another committee with yet another useless proposal, it is time for that country's citizens to express their dissatisfaction by getting rid of its useless representatives. A leading editorial in the *Independent* (24 February, 1990) deplored the increasing tendency of politicians to lie 'officially'—and then find another term for the lie to justify the practice, such as 'terminological inexactitudes', or 'economical with the truth'. After listing some of the major falsities perpetrated at the highest government level, it continued:

> These were some of the celebrated instances of what might be called intellectual dishonesty in the inner circles of the Thatcher administration. But perhaps it is the small change of half-truth, cumulatively piling up

over the weeks and months in the piggy banks of the public mind, that has done more than these few major furores to draw attention to the decline of respect for the truth under this Government.

Examples of the shifty suppression of the truth, the deft suggestion of the half-true, have been so numerous, from the Government in the House of Commons and even more from its secret briefers and nod-and-wink artists, that every connoisseur will have a choice collection . . .

It is over twenty years since the officially approved 19-nation Council of Europe provided its recommendations for dealing with the drug problem it labelled an 'epidemic'; yet few, if any, of them have been implemented. All of the nations represented have worse problems now than they had at the time the Report was compiled and presented; and all of them either grotesquely limit expenditure on the drug problem, or even curtail it.

US President Bush went to South America and formed an 'anti-drugs cartel' to interdict supplies, with three other Latin nations, but only spoke vaguely of addressing the real problem of 'demand' in the United States. Yet the British Home Secretary, David Waddington went to America, like his predecessor David Mellor, unsuccessfully looking for answers in the United States to the still unresolved addiction problem. Everybody involved knew that they were merely going through motions for publicity purpose, that they were unable or unwilling to do what was glaringly obvious—address the known spiritual 'sickness of society'.

In February, 1990, in the United Nations General Assembly, an international consensus was reached on a global programme to combat the drugs trade. According to a report in the *Independent* (23 February, 1990), 'The umbrella initiative on drugs has been called the most significant decision by the world body since the international human rights machinery was established in the 1970s.' Yet at that same gathering the British Foreign Secretary, Douglas Hurd

> . . . expressed alarm at the rise in the drug trade; he called on countries to enforce the 1988 Vienna Convention against drug trafficking . . . He was critical of the resources which have been committed to the three existing UN anti-drug bodies, however, and said that 'a single, unified body should be established to tackle the problem with a single, full-time head'.

Coming from a British representative of a government that has resisted the recommended idea of 'a single unified body, with a single head' to deal with its own drug problem, that was an exercise in unmitigated gall.

At a time when the nations of Europe are throwing off the yoke of an inadequate Marxist political and social system by means of committed Christians, it will be an ironic historical footnote if neither Britain nor America can find the will to jettison an equally inadequate secular democracy in order to restore Christian values. For it was the obscure Christian Lech Walesa who took on the might of the oppressive Communist regime in Poland. It was the little-known Christian pastor, Tomas Vasary, who was responsible for the revolution in Rumania. It was the Christian pastors who opened the churches to the young protesters who launched the revolution against Honecker's corrupt regime in East Germany. It was the Christians in churches in Czechoslovakia, Lithuania, Latvia, Estonia, Ukraine who marched against the oppressions and tyranny of their Communist leaders. It was the Communist Nelson Mandela who went into prison for almost thirty years, who came out of it a born-again Christian to impress the world with hope of a solution in South Africa.

It is revolution—not revival, not renewal, not reform—that Christians call for. Revolution is not a seventeenth- or nineteenth-century political weapon, but a Judaeo-Christian historical spiritual concept. God, not the French Marat or German Marx, was the first revolutionary. It was, and is, God who demands 'total change'—the meaning of 'revolution'. Conversion and repentance—God's work of salvation in the hearts of men and women—mean 'to turn round', or 'change direction'.

God says: 'When the vessel is marred in the hands of the potter, he smashes it, and makes it again as seems good to the potter to make it. Can I not deal with you as this potter does? Like clay in the hand of the potter so are you in my hands.' It is little wonder, therefore, that it is Christians who were, and still are, behind all meaningful revolutions in the West— French, British and American in the earlier centuries, and East European and African in the twentieth century.

But it needs a *spiritual* revolution in the nation! It is evident from the attitudes and policies of a variety of governments over the past two decades of increasing drugs crises that they are only prepared to address the cosmetic factor of interdicting the supplies of illicit drugs into their countries, or make half-hearted attempts to confiscate profits. Alcohol will not be touched, cigarettes may be tentatively restricted by increase of taxes, marijuana might be legalised if there is enough public pressure; but heroin, cocaine, and pharmaceutical products, in the vested interests of prescribing doctors, profitable corporations and powerful criminals, are issues which are too sensitive for politicians seeking votes to keep them in positions of power.

Addicts are not 'cured' until there is healing in body, mind and *spirit* of those who previously were unable to function responsibly or adequately in society because of chemical abuse. This involves a comprehension of, and a demonstrated capacity to put into effect, a new philosophy of life which is adequate to the addict's chosen environment — so that they are no longer in bondage to any form of chemical or behavioural addiction, but can live with freedom, peace, joy and love in family and community.

That is the responsibility of the Church, its primary message. The Old Testament prophet Jeremiah addressed his nation, Israel, with the words of God at a time of national crisis:

> If at any time I announce that a nation or a kingdom is to be uprooted, torn down and destroyed, and if that nation I warned repents of its evil, then I will relent and not inflict on it the disaster I had planned. And if at another time I announce that a nation or kingdom is to be built up and planted, and if it does evil in my sight and does not obey me, then I will reconsider the good I had intended to do for it . . . So turn from your evil ways, *each one of you*, and reform your ways and your actions . . . (our italics)

'Blessed is the nation whose God is the Lord . . . our heart shall rejoice in Him.' The word 'rejoice' means glad, merry, JOY. The Paradise Factor. Wherever there is a Bible there is a definition of the Paradise Factor in some way. The gospel message is of 'JOY unspeakable and full of glory'. The kingdom of God is not in meat and drink, but righteousness, peace and JOY. There is JOY in heaven over every sinner that repents. 'These things,' said Jesus, 'I have spoken to you, that my JOY might remain in you and your JOY might be full.' The kingdom of God is not in words, but in POWER. The last encouraging words of Jesus to the doomed John the Baptist regarding the true signs of His Messiahship were '. . . the blind see, the lame walk, the lepers are healed, the gospel is preached to the poor'. The true message of the Church is DELIVERANCE—from sickness to health, from bondage to freedom, from darkness to light. The Paradise Factor.

But it is not enough to be a professing Christian and expect to be able to provide a theoretical reply from a series of selected Bible verses. Nor even to be an evangelical, church-going, prayer-meeting-attending Christian; because, as has been noted, ritualisms—whether of the religious kind, or charity or social or political gatherings, or cult-communities, or even AA meetings—are also likely to be just behavioural addictive substitutes. One noted authority has written:

> The crucial point in judging the benefits of involvement in a group is whether the involvement is an end in itself. If it is, it can be an equivalent to the drug or other unhealthy habit it purports to cure. This is the danger of any group which claims that permanent membership in it is the only solution to the problem it is organised to combat . . . Membership in groups organised to combat addiction can itself be addictive if it limits participants to one lifestyle, one set of associations and one way of thinking and acting.
>
> There is another type of group that is rarely tried in our society. It involves, not the formation of groups on the basis of common addictions, but the use of existing units such as family or work groups . . . While working together on common problems of one person among them, friends and kin can serve as 'therapists' for one another . . .

In his book *God and Revolution* the theological writer Jurgen Moltman warns Christians talking about 'spiritual revolution':

> The theology of revolution is certainly no theology for bishops, but a lay theology for Christians who are suffering and struggling in the world. On the other hand, it must be said that there will be no 'theology of revolution'

> until there is a revolution in theology. *As long
> as Christians refrain from acting in a revolutionary
> way they have no right to be making theological
> declarations about revolution. Neither does the
> church have a right to a 'theology of revolution' in
> the world if it is not engaged in its own radical
> transformation.* It is totally inauthentic for the
> church to speak out and act against the
> economic alienation of man without struggling
> against the spiritual alienation which it itself
> propagates . . . (our italics)

Is this why the Church's leaders are silent at this time of
national crisis and unprecedented opportunity? Is there an
institutional guilt complex about the condition of the
Church and the lack of will to correct the ills? If Presidential
and political aspirants are aware of the nations' crises, and yet
can only propose inadequate law-enforcement solutions, the
Church leaders should be prominently proposing alternative
treatment and rehabilitation solutions. It was Christians who
gave the nation its first hospitals. It was the Salvation Army
who first cared for alcoholics. It was a Christian who began
Alcoholics Anonymous. It was a Christian pastor, Dave
Wilkerson, who began the Teen Challenge drug treatment
programme over twenty years ago.

There is no need for the true Christian Church at large
to be apologetic or modest about its potential for contribution
at this time of crisis. Several Presidents of the United States,
with all the power of the nation behind them, have been
unable to make any impact on the drug problem.

When John F. Kennedy became President he convened
a White House Conference on Drug Abuse under the
chairmanship of his brother, the then Attorney General
Robert Kennedy, to do something about the drug problem—
without success. President Lyndon Johnson created a single
unified organisation to deal with the growing drug problem,
the Bureau of Narcotics and Dangerous Drugs. He was

followed by President Richard Nixon, who declared drug abuse 'a rising sickness in our land', and continued: 'Within the last decade the abuse of drugs has grown from being essentially a local police problem into a serious threat to the personal health and safety of millions of Americans.' But still to no effect. President Gerald Ford said that 'conditions are worsening, and the gains of prior years are being eroded'. President Carter appointed a close colleague and friend, Presidential aide Dr Peter Bourne, as Director of the Office of Drug Abuse Policy, and he concluded: 'As long as there is a market in the world, and immense profit to be made, traffickers will always be able to find sites for cultivation despite our most vigorous efforts to suppress it.' In 1986 President Ronald Reagan and his wife, Nancy, went on television together to call for 'a national crusade against drugs'; and we have quoted the official statements of failure earlier in this book under President George Bush. President Clinton, in his first official budget, cut both finance and personnel from the government's drug advisory committee, and did not once address the drug problem in his first year of office.

But one willing clergyman attached to a voluntary agency is not contribution enough. One church of a single denomination in a community is not involvement enough. One sermon at a time of media publicity is not prophetic enough. One article on the national menace of the drug problem in a Christian publication is not concern enough.

If hundreds of noted church leaders can be found, at a time of a nation at war, to bless departing regiments of soldiers, or armoured instruments of war, why, at a time of a 'war on drugs', can no leading churchman be found to bless or encourage such front-line mobilisation of 'soldiers of the cross'? If hundreds of Christians can be mobilised to demonstrate against abortion clinics, why are there no Christian demonstrations against 'the world's worst social problem'—drugs? Why are there no Christian demonstrations *declaring the solution*—the Paradise Factor? The apathy and disinterest that has been manifested until the nation is at the point of being held hostage by unscrupulous criminals, uncaring politicians, uninformed doctors, unsuccessful police and uninvolved ecclesiasts must be brought to an end. It is time for national reflection, national repentance, and national conversion. It is time for a spiritual revolution.

The nation does not need a new defence programme, or a new foreign policy, or a new social agenda, or a new environmental emphasis. The nation needs a new spiritual revolution. The need for a spiritual revolution in Western nations is Alexandr Solzhenitsyn's prophetic message. As he argues in his books and broadcasts, spiritual solutions to society's problems—and the necessary discarding of the useless materialist substitutes now being promulgated from a variety of self-interested sources—result from true expressions of Christian freedom. This Christian freedom is very different from the unlimited freedom so beloved of the Western intellectual, and the Marxist concept of freedom as the acceptance of the yoke of necessity; Christian freedom is *self-restriction*—discipline of the self for the sake of others.

The tragic history of humankind is that they are reluctant to surrender to the beneficent contingent freedom offered by God, but instead rebel against the limitations that come with it. It is like wanting to drive in a city where no one submits to the traffic signals—sooner or later there is bound to be a crash.

In his great epistle to the Romans, the Apostle Paul describes the state of nations and individuals who ignore, neglect or reject God's offer of grace and mercy, love and forgiveness:

> God's anger is revealed from heaven against all
> the sin and evil of the people whose evil ways
> prevent the truth from being known. God
> punishes them, because what can be known
> about God is made plain to them, for God

himself has made it plain. Ever since God created the world, his invisible qualities, both his eternal power and divine nature, have been clearly seen; they are perceived in the things that God has made. So these people have no excuse at all! They know God, but they do not give him the honour that belongs to him, nor do they thank him. Instead, their thoughts have become complete nonsense, and their empty minds are filled with darkness. They say they are wise, but they are fools . . .

Because these people refuse to keep in mind the true knowledge about God, he has given them over to corrupted minds, so that they do the things they should not do. They are filled with all kinds of wickedness . . .

But the Apostle Paul did not just leave it there. In the course of his majestic epistle he goes on to describe how those 'corrupt, senseless, debased minds' can be transformed (our italics): 'Do not conform yourselves to the standards of this world, but *let God transform you inwardly by a complete change of your mind.* Then you will be able to know the will of God—what is good and pleasing to him and is perfect.' Revolution! Paradise!

C. S. Lewis wrote in *Surprised by Joy*:

We are, as Newman said, rebels who must lay down our arms . . . To render back the will which we have so long claimed as our own, is in itself, whenever and however it is done, a grievous pain . . . To surrender a self-will inflamed and swollen with years of usurpation is a kind of death . . .

It is not that the problem of addictions is new to this generation alone, or even to this century. Drunkenness is as ancient as Noah. Ritualism as a replacement for spirituality is as old as the Jews. There were probably more addicts and alcoholics in the nineteenth century than there are now. The critical factor at this stage of the twentieth century is the organised exploitation of political and spiritual weaknesses of societies by criminals, and the ineffectiveness of any form of government to seriously address the root causes of the problem. What changed all of the circumstances of the past—from Noah to nineteenth century—was a new infusion of spirituality into the lives of individuals and communities and nations by courageous and outspoken spiritual men and women.

Now that the Western nations, at the close of the twentieth century, are seeing something of the consequences of their neglect or rejection of God in their daily family lives, they are being brought face to face with hard decisions: to continue on the downward path to more of the same, or to turn from their obsessive self-interest to God-recognition. It involves more than mere regret for pursuing a wrong course; it means repentance for choosing a wrong guide in the first place. Repentance is a spiritual act, and it is the first step God requires in an individual or nation who turns to Him for help.

The historical churches have quiescently accepted the marginalisation of their spiritual witness, except for ecclesiastical vested interests and sociological identity, and inevitably have been replaced as spiritual counsellors by secular psychiatrists. The secular rationalisms of the humanists and psychiatrists have left an empty void in the daily lives of people, and with the institutional churches also distanced from the specific issues of life by liturgical ritualisms, all that is left in the daily lives of the population is emptiness and meaninglessness.

A spiritual revolution will require self-judgement first at the House of God, a transformation of the people of God, before the nation can be changed. Studies in Britain and the United States have shown that there are as many Christians as non-Christians dependent on some form of chemical substance—caffeine or tranquillisers, barbiturates or nicotine, if not alcohol or cocaine. Ritualistic church attendance, with preaching and prayer stimulation as an end in themselves, is just as addictive as gambling with horses, cards or bingo.

Preachers who offer a 'high'—to be 'kissed by God'—through prayer, speaking in tongues, and being 'slain in the Spirit', instead of a disciplined walk in obedience and holiness with God, are as professionally assured as doctors or dealers that their prescribed 'products' work—and are just as unscrupulous and delusory. Millions of professing Christians are addicted to a counterfeit stimulation because they have not been told about the real experience—the true Paradise Factor. They have looked through the window into Paradise; they know it exists. A behavioural formula has reached them from pulpit or radio or television screen, and the tantalising feathery tendrils of paradisal experience have brushed across the tedious mediocrity of their lives. They spend ten, twenty, a hundred dollars a time for more of the same; but the only Paradise they experience is a Christianised television chat show or amusement park. They don't find their Christian preachers there, though; because they and their wives and families are usually elsewhere chasing their own versions of illusory paradise.

The institutional churches of every persuasion—Orthodox, Catholic, Protestant, conservative, liberal, evangelical, or fundamentalist, as they are presently constituted—are not equipped to deal with the current drug problem. While many of them have marriage counselling groups, Samaritan counselling groups, family counselling groups, youth counselling groups, young married counselling groups and so on, very few have addiction counselling groups—and where they have they are usually feeble imitations of AA groups and for their own church members.

When addicts go to churches they are faced with the usual 'religious sandwich' of church services: hymn, prayer, hymn, reading, hymn, sermon, hymn, prayer, benediction. The hymns are usually more ancient than modern, the lyrics obscure in meaning, and the sermons filled with arcane bewildering jargon. Members of the churches mix freely and vivaciously with each other, sometimes they will shake hands in friendly greeting with a visitor—and the addict is left to go on his or her way without help for their urgent need.

There are three institutions provided by God for the proper ordering of society: the State, the Church, and the Family.[2] Faced with the present crisis situation where a nation-state has a major social problem threatening its citizens, and where the State and the Church are not making adequate provision, the only solution is for the afflicted individual families or sympathetic associates to take matters into their own hands.

The criminal organisations of the world are committed to exploiting the drug trade by every means in their power—and they have the astronomical profits from the trade to help them defy governments. They will move ruthlessly from nation to nation, from coast to interior, from cities to towns to villages, from mansions to ghettoes, from sports stadia to schools, from Wall Street to Skid Row, in their implacable pursuit of profits and power. Their wealth ensures that presidents of countries and banks and corporations, police commissioners as well as police constables, politicians and journalists, judges and lawyers, publishers and writers and film-makers, and lobbyists of all kinds, are paid enough to keep the astronomical drug profits safely flowing—and to maintain and even increase the nation's bondage to drugs of all kinds.

If the State does not care, then the Church should. If the historical Church does not care, then individual Christians should rise up in protest. What use is a religion if its prophets do not speak up for the oppressed, the poor, the sick? What kind of Christian are you if you are not doing something in your country, your community, your street, your family, to combat a devilish enemy threatening your very

---

2. See *God and the Family*, by George N. Patterson (to be published).

existence? How many are going to be praying in churches this week:

> Our Father in heaven,
> hallowed be your Name,
> your kingdom come,
> your will be done
> on earth as it is in heaven . . .
> and lead us not into temptation,
> but deliver us from the evil one . . . ?

There never was a better time, nor a greater cause, for the Christian messenger. Billions of people in hundreds of countries know there is a 'Paradise Factor', for they have experienced it; but they also know it does not satisfactorily exist in chemicals, or rituals, or people. They want to know where to find it in full fruition as they have touched it in fleeting fantasy; and they want it here and now.

It is available. *Detoxification* from all forms of chemical addiction in ten days, without supplementary drugs, is now possible with NeuroElectric Therapy—we know this from independent scientific research conducted in Britain and the United States. *Rehabilitation* from all forms of chemical and behavioural addiction, to follow detoxification, is now possible, as we have outlined in this book and elsewhere.

The solution to the addiction problem, the Paradise Factor, is provided. Its use and acceptance is up to you.

The Jeremiah Manifesto of Spiritual Revolution

> It is better to have no king than a bad king. It is better to have no rulers than have rulers whose personal ambitions are at variance with the wellbeing of the people. It is better to be without civil authorities than have civil authorities whose policies replace spiritual

values with material goals. It is better to have no prophets than have prophets who preach platitudes and seek personal power. It is better to have no prophets than have prophets who cultivate popularity and who turn divine truths into hackneyed truisms. It is better to have no priests than have priests who care more for their religious system than for the souls of the people. It is better to have no priests than have priests whose beliefs can be altered by false idols and ideologies. It is better to have no priests than have priests who have never personally met nor talked with God. It is better to have no Word of God than a Word of God misconstrued, misinterpreted and misapplied.

Jeremiah, chapters 22 and 23

APPENDIX

Report of the Council of Europe (Strasbourg, 1970) Recommendations

*I*n the light of the information received from the national health administrations and of the findings by the members of the team, it appears that the spread of drug dependence has reached epidemic proportions in the 19 countries surveyed.

This epidemic is still increasing and, in view of the lack of complete, accurate and up-to-date information, there is no possibility of forecasting its course, dimensions and duration.

Bearing in mind the importance of drug dependence in Europe and in view of the fact that:

(a) drug dependence is spreading alarmingly and rapidly amongst juveniles (in some European cities at least 25 per cent of juvenile groups are at present involved) and that new patterns in drug dependence among juveniles are developing;

(b) drug dependence is increasing in whole populations, especially dependence on those drugs which are not yet under international narcotics control;

(c) there is real danger of the formation of a whole sub-culture;

(d) there is a serious lack of information,

a detailed programme is needed if prevention and treatment are to be successful.

While considering that the actual facts of the problem are changing from month to month, the study group feels the necessity for carrying out further studies in the field and for taking immediate measures.

It therefore brings the following recommendations to the attention of the governments concerned:

Information

1. It is recommended that, in each member country, data relating to different types of drug dependence and the personnel status of the drug dependant should be collected on a local, national and European level, on the basis of a standardised questionnaire. Such a questionnaire should be drawn up under the responsibility of the Council of Europe. A regular exchange of information collected on the basis of such a questionnaire should be organised and maintained on local, national and European levels. In every country an appropriate organ should be set up to collect and evaluate the information and to advise the government in so far as is necessary.

Research

2. With a view to prevention and treatment in each country concerned, experts in the field of drug dependence should be appointed to carry out prospective epidemiological studies and other research projects (i.e. psychic and physical dependence, biochemistry and pharmacological aspects, personality of the drug dependant, group dynamics of adolescent drug users, new methods of education of the public and the professions concerned with this problem).

Treatment

3. Considering the lack of adequate treatment facilities for drug dependants, hospital beds should be made available as urgently as possible. In addition, new special institutions for treatment and after-care should be set up for rehabilitation. Particular attention should be paid to the training of specialised staff able to carry out the treatment.

Prevention

4. In each of the countries concerned, continuous prospective research should be undertaken to detect from the outset new trends in drug abuse, with a view to taking immediate and coordinated preventative measures.

5. Public opinion should be kept currently informed of the dangers of drug dependence. Private agencies should be established with governmental assistance to advise on and prepare material, designed for the information of the population. Well-conceived educational programmes are essential for successful prevention through mass media, schools, clubs, in cooperation with juveniles, parents, teachers, psychologists, social workers, psychiatrists and ex-addicts. Supervised studies should check the efforts and the success of preventative endeavours.

6. Consultative centres should be available for juveniles who are anxious to obtain professional advice on and assistance in their efforts to free themselves from the danger of a tendency towards drug dependence, without fear of penal prosecution.

7. While the drug-abuser—whether a beginner or already dependent—is a medical problem, the drug trafficker is a legal one and severe punitive measures should be taken against anyone who derives profit from the craving of the dependent individual or seduces the uninitiated to become drug dependent.

Coordination

8. An appropriate centre in one of the member states of the Council of Europe should be entrusted with:

    (a) the collection and dissemination of information;

    (b) the coordination of national research at an international level and promotion of joint research;

    (c) new proposals for research, prevention and treatment programmes.

INDEX

DR MEG

Meg Patterson

'*I had no great ambition . . . to be a self-centred career woman. I did know that I wanted something meaningful . . . challenging, in which I could use the skills God had given me,*' said Meg on becoming a Fellow of the Royal College of Surgeons at the age of twenty-five, one of only twenty women who had ever become Fellows in Edinburgh at that time. An unexpected meeting—some would call it chance, but Meg's faith taught her otherwise—led her to a post at Ludhiana Christian Medical College in India. Her marriage to George Patterson, a journalist already known for his work in Tibet, at first seemed impossible because of their apparently irreconcilable vocations, but they knew that God would weave their separate lives into His purposes, so they went ahead into an unknown future. Work in India, Nepal and Honk Kong led Meg away from surgery and into the development of a unique treatment for chemical dependency.

Meg's autobiography is largely an account of her lifelong struggle to have her revolutionary treatment recognised and financially supported in Britain and the USA. It is an exciting, often humorous and always inspiring story of unswerving commitment and perseverance, despite frankly admitted periods of despondency, and after forty years Meg concludes that: '*We were all pilgrims moving on . . . but our whole family had been brought into a glorious venture with God that no one in their wildest imagination could have foreseen.*'

Catalogue Number YB 9241   £4.50

THE POWER FACTOR
The Key to Conquering Addiction

George and Meg Patterson

> ### *CAN YOU BE SET FREE?*
> ### *IS THERE AN ANSWER?*

What you want, what you need, is—**POWER**. Power to break the habit or practice. Power to deal with the problems that drove you to them in the first place. Power to heal the broken relationships with your family. Power to do something constructive in society. Power to change 'the sorry scheme of things entire, and mould it nearer to our heart's desire'. Power to know and love the worthy God.

> ### *IS THERE SUCH A POWER?*
> ### *WHERE IS IT TO BE FOUND?*
> ### *HOW CAN IT BE OBTAINED?*
> ### *HOW CAN YOU BE SET FREE?*

The answers to these and many more questions are what *The Power Factor* is all about.

This book is an attempt to make a wider contribution to the solutions necessary in making, not just addicts, but a sick society, whole in body, mind *and spirit*.

Catalogue Number YB 9111   £3.50

THE CHINA PARADOX

George Patterson

For more than five thousand years China has produced legendary figures in philosophy, science and the arts—but none in religion. Numerically the largest nation in the world, China has never developed a religion in the true sense of the term: to 're-ligature' the human soul with God. Confucianism and Taoism taught a way of life, Buddhism was imported from India, and over thousands of years the Chinese people superstitiously and indiscriminately worshipped nature, spirits and dead ancestors.

Of the only two major belief systems which dominated China, one was ancient and spiritual and one was modern and godless—Christianity and Marxism—and both were borrowed from the West. Ironically and paradoxically, it was Christianity which paved the way for Marxism to become China's first national religion. It was in China's Christian schools and universities that the leaders of China's Marxism were educated in Western ideas.

In *The China Paradox* this fascinating historical phenomenon is portrayed with unique skill and insight by a Christian writer who watched at first hand the final death of Westernised Christianity and the rise of a dynamic Marxism; then watched the rise and spread of a revitalised biblical Christianity eventually survive and triumph over a dying Marxism.

In this book the author records the historic events which, after five decades of totalitarian Marxism, have led to Chinese Christians exceeding in numbers the active membership of the Chinese Communist Party which continues to rule China in 1989—the ultimate China paradox.

Catalogue Number YB 9320   £3.25